A Man's Guide
To Surviving Divorce, Breakups and Women in General

William Spriggs

ISBN:1466385308
ISBN-13:9781466385306

DEDICATION

This book is dedicated to every man who ever thought he was doing it right. It is
dedicated to every man who has ever been blindsided by a divorce or a breakup or by
a woman with whom he was in a relationship and had his little cherry red Kool aid
pump busted.

CONTENTS

I wrote this little book after my divorce. It helped me bring closure to some of the emotions and feelings that would crop up from time to time. It is by no means legal advice or a divorce "kit" type how to book. God knows there are plenty of those out there. There are also plenty of books on how to get your wife back, stop your divorce, etc. Nothing wrong with those books either. This book is to help you understand the emotions you are feeling and to help you deal with them in a productive manner. Most of this stuff is common sense; the problem is that most guys getting dumped by the woman they love seldom exercise common sense.

This little book is designed to help you realize that your life is not over now that she has decided to leave you. It is based on common sense and personal experience. There is an old saying, "Life is hard, and it's harder if you're stupid." Most men who are experiencing the destruction of the family they loved so deeply aren't stupid, just so emotionally off balance that they make bad choices. I am not trying to discourage you from trying to get your wife back. I don't think I can. What I do hope to do is help you recover when it doesn't work, to give you reasons why it is going to be alright.

In this book I also address the reasons the divorce happened in the first place. I am going to explain to you the reason for the rising divorce rate and the culture that has created the current mindset that makes it almost inevitable. Finally I give a concrete plan to help men reclaim the civilization that has been destroyed by the social and cultural forces that destroy marriage and families

I will then tell what you need to know to understand women. Yes, Virginia, they can be understood and are really very simple creatures, despite their self pronouncements otherwise.

Some reading this book might choose to label me a misogynist. Nothing could be further from the truth. I don't hate women; I do hate what our culture has become and the effect it has had on our relationships and our families. Some reading the first draft felt there were parts that were "angry". In writing this I no doubt loosened some cobwebs of anger and sadness and a few other emotions. I assure you that those emotions that have been dealt with and were dealt with before I started pounding away at the keyboard.

A level of clarity and normalcy will eventually return to your mind and life. I wrote this book in order to help you expedite that process.

It is my sincere desire that this book helps you. It was written for that purpose.

I would like to thank all those who helped me through the rough spots when the big Divorce Bomb got dropped on me the second time. All of you know who you are and what you helped me see then, I now share with the readers.

Thanks.

How to Survive Your Divorce

(And women in general)

She just walked out. She packed her stuff and left and has told you she is filing for divorce, or wants to call it quits, an end to the relationship, break up with you, etc. etc. blah, blah, blah. The marriage is over and the girl is moving on without you. There are scores of books, both online and in print that will tell you how to get her back and save your marriage.

I won't tell you how to do that. I am here to tell you that in most cases you have been duped and played and the best thing that ever happened to you was her walking out. Most of what I am going to tell you in this book goes against all conventional wisdom from the popular media, most religious institutions and from the so called "experts". Once I had recovered somewhat from my own divorce and was beginning to learn and apply the lessons I will share with you, a friend commented to me, "If most men were honest, they would love to be in your position right now."

I am no expert, experts built the Titanic and an amateur built the Ark. I am a guy who lived through it not once, but twice, dumb I know. I am a guy who got to forty, looked around and said, "Wow, I'm single again. My wife left me for another guy, I am looking at poverty via child support and I am sleeping alone." At first, I panicked. I was scared. It hurt like no other pain I had ever felt. I wanted to die, to melt into oblivion.

I had several friends who told me I'd be fine. One of them told me, "Bill you are a survivor, no matter what happens, you will come out standing tall and ahead of the game." What my friends told me was exactly true. I am going to help the rest of you men who just got the news. I am going to tell you how to survive women in general and a divorce in particular.

This is going to be an eye opening experience for some of you, for others it will be a confirmation of what you have suspected all along. This information might even upset or anger some of you. Good if it does. What I am going to tell you will be attacked by women and some men as crazy.

Most of the information at the front of this book has to do with married men and how to get through the initial stages of becoming divorced. If you are single and ending a relationship with a woman you were dating or simply cohabitating with, the information you will need to understand why she is leaving comes later. If you are mystified at the behavior of women in Western civilization I will explain in the final section how this state of affairs came to be and what men individually and collectively can do to restore order to our own lives and civilization as a whole.

This book wasn't written for women. It is written for men going through divorce by a man who went through a divorce. This book wasn't written for men who are planning on leaving their wives in order to "find themselves" or pursue an affair with another woman. If you are a woman whose husband has left you and you happen to be reading this, flip to the last section on "why" and you might understand some of the factors that caused him to leave. If you are a man reading this and you are having an affair with a married woman, helping to wreck a family, the only advice I have for you is to just remember, you don't plant carrots and get corn.

This book is short. It is short and concise for a reason. You are a man, and men have things to do. We don't have time to waste reading a bunch of touchy feely psycho babble crap. We have places to be and stuff to get done. It is short because I want you to start living, to ease the pain in your soul and get on with your life.

SHE'S GONE

You never saw it coming. You might have suspected it, you might have had some idea that things weren't right, *something* was wrong, but you just figured the two of you would get through it like you always did and life would go on. Men get comfortable. As long as things are going well enough, we often forget that a woman has a set of needs so totally divorced from our reality as to almost not exist. There is a reason there is a huge porn industry for men, but no romance novels. Most men don't get this, later we cover the why of that. Right now, you need to understand exactly where you are in the scheme of your relationship.

The statistics are pretty clear, in modern America, women file for divorce over seventy per cent of the time. Wow. The old idea that men run off and abandon a loving supportive wife, leaving her for a younger woman and a sports car is plain wrong. Nope, you were a good loving husband who just wanted to come home to his wife and family every night. You didn't go to the tavern or corner bar, you went home. You worked hard and were dedicated to your family. Now, for a reason you cannot understand or comprehend, your wife, the woman you loved and wanted to grow old with is gone. You weren't a drunk, a cheater or abuser, but still, she decided to leave. The trend of women walking away from an established marriage is growing every year. There is even a clinical term for it in the psychology and marriage counseling circles; Michele Weiner Davis calls it the "walk away wife" syndrome. This trend is so pervasive and common that there is even a "term" for it.

I am here to tell you, you are not alone. It has happened to seventy out of one hundred guys who are getting divorced if we are to believe the numbers.

It will continue to happen. Right now you just want to know why and you want to know how to fix it, how to get her back and fix and heal your family. I am here to tell you that chances are, this isn't going to happen. Sorry, buy all the books on how to heal the relationship and get your wife back you want to. Go ahead; give it the old college try. I will tell you that the deck is stacked against you in a big way.

I am going to get in depth into the "whys" later. Right now, I am going to tell you that you have to accept the fact that she is never, ever going to come back and if she does, by that time there is a chance that her self destructive behavior will have affected you to the point that you won't want her back. You have to let this reality seep into your subconscious mind. You have to pound it into your conscious mind. It hurts, I know it hurts. Let it hurt but accept it:

SHE IS NOT COMING HOME

She is gone. Sorry friend. It's reality, a reality you need to embrace. If you are still wearing it, pull your wedding band off and put it in a box or move it to your right hand until the divorce is legally over. Let it symbolize the death of the relationship because that is exactly what has happened. You must accept this as stone cold, hard fact.

If you don't accept it, you will do and say some pretty stupid things. You will push her further away and make her angrier, allowing her to emotionally and mentally justify the destruction of your assets and your life and the alienation of your children..

I was a Drill Sergeant at Ft. Knox Kentucky for two years. During that time I helped train approximately 900 soldiers. Inevitably, during the first few hectic weeks of basic training, when we Drill Sergeants were leaning pretty heavily on the troops, a recruit would come to my office and tell me he had made a mistake. He wanted to go home, this Army stuff just wasn't for him. I hesitated the first time this happened and wanted to help the soldier to be.

5

My Drill Sergeant buddy sitting at his desk casually shining a pair of boots, waited to see how I would handle the situation. I started trying to reason with the young man. My Drill Sergeant partner in crime finally interrupted and said to the Private, "Did you sign on the line at the recruiter's office? Did you raise your hand and swear the oath of enlistment?" The recruit said, "Yes Drill Sergeant." "Then get your ass out of my office and go start figuring out how to soldier instead of wasting my time wanting to undo reality. You are here now, deal with it."

Whether you wanted it or not, whether you asked for it or had it coming, you are getting left, dumped. Reality sucks sometimes, but it is reality nonetheless. The fact is, she has already divorced you with her heart, her mind and probably her body. All that is left for her to do is make it "legal." She has decided the marriage is over. She might not tell *YOU* that, but if she is talking about separation or has told you she wants a divorce, she might be there physically, but her heart is no longer yours. Don't kid yourself with rationalizations, advice from well meaning friends, family or religious counselors. She is leaving and there is no reason to believe she will change her mind or more importantly, her heart.

In a bit I will explain how her leaving is going to be one of the best things that ever happened if you let it. Right now I cannot emphasize enough that you have to accept it. Before we move on, I want to address some of the things that are going through your mind, some objections you are going to have to my line of reasoning. I know you love your wife. I know you just want to be a husband and a father and grow old with the woman you fell in love with all those years ago. In order to hold onto that dream, that love, you are going to come up with emotionally based objections to letting her go. Some of these are of your own making; some of these are products of society. Let us address a few of them.

1. I Love Her

Of course you do. That is why you married her in the first place, I hope. But guess what, **she no longer loves you**, if she ever did. She might be saying with her mouth "I love you" but what are her actions saying? *That* is the test, deeds not words. If she really loved you the way she says she does, she wouldn't have packed her stuff, taken the kids and moved out or be threatening to move out, she wouldn't have filed for the divorce or recommended separation. She would, if she really loved you, be making an attempt to fix the problems between you and if she is seeing someone else, well, she wouldn't be, *IF* she really loved you. If she is saying that she loves

6

you and that this is hurting her, she's crying, acting all emotional, etc. it is more than likely out of guilt. Genuine love doesn't quit, it doesn't bail when things get hard or there are problems. She is in love with herself right now and no one but herself.

Sorry bud, but that is the simple truth of the matter. She no longer loves you. So, why are you still holding on to the romanticized notion that somehow your love for her ought to be undying and that your heart ought to be a doormat for her to wipe her feet on as she walks out the door? Let me shock you here, love has nothing to do with marriage. Love is a nice component of marriage, but so are trust and honesty. If she says she loves you but is leaving, has left, is sleeping with someone else, has a "friend" or is listening to someone else and taking their advice instead of her husband's; **she is lying when she says she loves you**. Chances are her idea of love is a romantic myth so divorced from the reality of genuine mature love that she honestly believes she loves you. The difference is, mature adult love, grounded in reality, seldom engages in behavior that is destructive to the object of the love.

I will discuss our messed up notions of love and marriage later, right now you have got to let go of the notion that because you love her and had a life with her, she is worth continuing to love. I know it hurts. Let it hurt, but stop internalizing and holding on to that unreturned love.

2. I Need Her

Yup, a part of you does. A part of you had roots that grew down together and wrapped around each other. She handled some parts of the day to day operation of the marriage. You do need her, emotionally, mentally and physically. You need her, but here is the reality, **she no longer needs or wants to need *you* or wants you to need her**. She has flipped a switch somewhere deep down inside and turned off that connection to you. You are dying inside right now because you are suffering a deficit of the subtle power that being a part of a couple provides. She has uncoupled the two of you. One of the reasons for any tears she might be shedding now is because she feels that loss as well. The difference is she has made a plan to live with the deficit or has found a replacement.

As much as you think you need her, how did you manage to survive before she came along? Think about it. You were cruising along, living your life and then you met her, fell "in love" and got married. Remember when you were a kid and thought that girls were yucky and had cooties? Remember what your life was like before you met her. Were you generally happy? Stop lying to yourself and admit it, for the most part you were. If you got married because you wanted to be "happy" or in order to "not be alone" you made a mistake in the first place.

The bottom line: **you don□t need her as much as you think you do**.

3. I Don□t Want Anyone Else

No you don't. Not right now anyway. There are six billion or so people in the world. Half of those six billion are women. Three billion women in the world and you are fixated on a woman who no longer wants you. If there were only a billion women and five billion men, I could see your point. It would suck to have lost a woman under those circumstances, maybe. Trust me, right now there is at least one single woman sizing you up, having heard about your pending or finalized divorce. Right now, that romanticized notion of love you have been brainwashed with is telling you to hold on to the love you have for only one out of three billion women on the planet that you could give that love to.

One out of three billion, no woman alive is worth *that* much of your time and energy especially if she broke the marriage contract in the first place. Would you pour energy and time and worry into anything else like that? The only exception I can think of would be my children. Everything else is replaceable. What if your employer cheated you and broke the terms of the employment contract? I bet a nickel you'd quit and find another job at the first opportunity. She left. You can and more than likely will find a replacement and if you are smart, you'll find a better replacement.

Right now you only think you don't want anyone else. Trust me, over time, when the hurt and pain starts to subside and you actually get to looking around, you will find that there are hundreds of available women in your area and even overseas if you choose that can make a better wife for you than your ex could ever hope to be.

4. What About Losing my Children?

This is the toughest one. No doubt, faced with the prospect of not being a full time father to one's children is the hardest part of divorce. It is almost, *almost*, worth fighting tooth and nail to save the marriage for the sake of the children and if a man decides to fight for his family and to win back his wife's heart for his children's sake, no one with any sense would be critical of that. But I want you to consider this for a moment, especially if you have sons, do you really want your children to have memories of dad begging mom to come home? Do you think it is healthy for your sons and daughters to see you as a sniveling, crying lump of emasculation?

Your sons will be the kind of men they see you being. Your daughters will look for a man just like you when they start looking for a man. Do you want your sons to get walked on and mistreated by a woman? Do you want your daughters to think that being a doormat is what a man is supposed to be? There is more at stake here than your spending time with your kids. I'll address the kids and divorce again; I'm not done with this subject by a long shot.

In any event, whether you waste time trying to win her back or not, the reality is she is breaking up your family. She has placed her own happiness above the happiness and emotional and mental well being of her children. *She* is doing this, not you. Do you really want a woman like that around your children full time? She will attempt to justify her actions by telling herself that the children will be just fine. She is lying to herself but there is nothing you can do about it. Do not use the children as a reason to ask her to come home. If she genuinely cared about the welfare of the children, and you aren't a worthless drunken bum who beat the family on a regular basis, she would have stayed and worked things out with you for them. If children are the highest alleged priority in a woman's life, and she is leaving despite the ton of research proving the harmful effect divorce has on children, her selfishness ought to be apparent.

I am going to ask you to do a hard thing. I am going to ask you, for the sake of your own emotional and mental well being to divorce the idea of your children from your wife. This is hard, I know. But the reality is that she is the one removing them from your life against your will. She is in effect emotionally kidnapping them. Is someone who would do that worth loving and trying to have a life with?

5. God is against divorce/ divorce is a sin

If you aren't a particularly religious person, or an atheist, this might not apply to you. Either way, I will bet that on some level, when you first found out it was happening, you lifted your eyes to the heavens and asked "why". The end of your marriage might even be a catalyst for you to question your faith. "Why" would a good, loving God allow this to happen? I told you, we'll get to the "whys". Right now let's address the religious objection.

Appendix A will provide you a detailed study of the subject of divorce in the Bible. I am not insensitive to the fact that there are dozens of religions and scores of Christian sects and denominations. I can only assume that a Muslim in Pakistan is not the primary audience of this book, neither is a Buddhist in Tibet. I feel that I can safely assume that most of those reading this will be living in Western civilization, a civilization whose cultural attitudes and norms have been shaped in part by the Bible. The Bible is full of stories and guidance of all types. For some it is a matter of firm conviction that they live by the precepts and principles in the Scripture. For some the Bible is just a good book, not really Divine but one that can be used as a guide to living a good life.

If this is a concern to you ask yourself what *God* says about marriage and divorce in the Bible. And not what a preacher or priest, as well meaning as they may be, or a church or denomination tells us God says. Chances are, the preacher is going home to his wife tonight and you will be sleeping alone. Go get counsel if you must from your pastor or priest, but don't let the guy heap a bunch of guilt on you for something so totally out of your control.

If this isn't your thing, don't bother with Appendix A. If it is, the principle is this; **God cannot and will not make or force anyone to love you**. He doesn't even make or force us to love Him. It violates His nature to force Himself on anyone. Marriage is supposed to be a contract between two people. It makes for a better marriage if our wives love us and we love them. Love is a strong indicator of a good marriage, but it is not a requirement for a good marriage. All of us have been told that we need to be "in love" to be married, but that is pretty much bunk, a myth created during the late middle ages. We are commanded to love our wives as Christ loved the Church, but we aren't commanded to be "in love". There is a difference and I'll explain that in a later section.

Go ahead and pray and ask God to heal your marriage and bring your wife back. It may or may not happen. God does work miracles, sometimes. But the reason we recognize those instances as "miracles" is because they are so rare. Do you get that? A miracle is a rare occurrence. With the divorce rate at 50%, and according to some, highest amongst evangelical Christians, a rare occurrence is exactly what you praying your wife back home will be. Once again, I'm not saying don't try it, I am saying that God won't force your wife to return, He doesn't operate that way.

Look, I know you are dying inside right now. I know you love your wife and cannot imagine how this happened, but it has. Don't delude yourself into rationalizing reasons to keep and hold false hope. The sooner you let go, the sooner you will begin to heal and get on with your life.

10

The fact of the matter is, she has already begun to divorce you from an emotional and mental standpoint. You are already divorced in a very real sense whether you realize it or not. She has begun to distance herself from you emotionally. Get that, if she has left, moved out, asked for a separation, etc. etc. you are divorced already. The paperwork is a formality. The court proceedings are just an opportunity for her to rake you over the coals and take your money and relegate you to a part time father.

PROTECT YOURSELF

You didn't ask for the divorce and the destruction of your family. She doesn't love you anymore in any way that actually matters and she isn't coming back. It doesn't matter how much you love her and miss her and need her. It doesn't matter that she was the woman you wanted to spend the rest of your life with. It doesn't matter that she is the mother of your children. She is divorcing you.

Until you accept this as a fact of life, you won't act on it as fact. If you show up for work on Monday and the boss tells you that you are fired, would you get up the next day and go to work there anyway, hoping that the company changes its mind and pays you at the end of the week? Of course you wouldn't. You'd get up the next day and go find another job. You might miss some of the people you worked with. You might miss what you actually did at work. Still, you wouldn't show up the next day because of what you would miss about the job. You would act in a manner consistent with the reality of the situation. You need to do the same now. No amount of wishing, hoping and praying is going to bring her back. *You can ignore reality; you cannot ignore the consequences of ignoring reality.*

I know you might be sitting here holding out some hope even after reading this. Fine, have all the hope you want, pray all you want, do what ever you think you need to do to win back her affection. Statistics tell us that, only about 15% of divorced couples ever reconcile and that is usually after an extended separation of five years or so. During that time usually both of the formerly married people have other relationships. Feel free to believe that

12

you are one of the exceptions, but in all REALITY, the numbers are against you. I could give you anecdotal stories from the men and women I have talked to that would verify the numbers, but at the end of the day, the numbers are exactly that, numbers, raw data. Once again, the data says she isn't coming home.

You hopefully have started to accept that your wife is gone. Even if you still want to try and bring her home, what I am about to tell you is very important. First, it will help you maintain your sanity and more importantly, your role as a man. Primarily, it will help you protect yourself and your children if the union produced any.

The most important part of all of this is that you act first and proactively in legal and financial terms regardless of how badly you might want her to come home. Your love for her compared to your money and time with the children are two completely different things. Don't allow the love and pain and hurt to cloud your common sense when it comes to protecting yourself.

Protect Yourself Legally

I have no doubt that most men, once they realize the divorce is actually happening, want it to be as amicable as possible. After all you love her; she's the mother of your children. Nice thought. Now, go hire a lawyer, a good one. What you might not realize is that 95% of the time, your wife has been planning on leaving you for a long time. She has been planning this, preparing for it mentally and emotionally while she was pretending everything was fine. Maybe when she was in the middle of having super hot sex with you; some part of her brain was looking around the bedroom figuring out what she wanted to take with her. While she was sitting at the table watching you scarf down your favorite meal, she was mentally dividing up the money. She has talked to a few of her friends about it, especially the man "friend". She has looked at the divorce laws, talked to a few women who have recently left their husbands and gotten all sorts of good advice on the best way to get out of your life, to in her mind, escape. She might have even hired a lawyer well in advance of dropping the divorce bomb on you.

DO NOT SIGN ANYTHING UNTIL YOU TALK TO AN ATTORNEY!!!!!!!!!!

Go out *right now* and find the toughest, meanest divorce lawyer you can. Find a woman if at all possible to represent you. Make this a priority. I can't and won't give you any specific legal advice. I'm not a lawyer, but I know how to use the phone book and so do you. Some people will tell you to go put several of the known blood suckers in town who practice family law on retainer so your soon to be ex can't. In most areas of the country, the lawyers are wise to this trick and will charge an exorbitant amount of money in order for you to do this. If you think you have enough money and can afford it, do it anyway. All she needs to do is find one really good family practice lawyer and she can wipe you out, even though she is the one walking away. I know it isn't fair. I'll explain in a later chapter why it isn't fair but it happens anyway. Know this for now, the Latin root for maternal and materialism are the same, "mater" or mother, i.e. female.

Once you decide on the lawyer and hire them, DO NOT talk to your soon to be ex wife about any legal issues. Be as nice as you can to her and then refer her and her questions to your lawyer. Why? If you have children with this woman, she is going to be in your life for a long, long time. It is in your best interest and in the best interest of your children for you to be as nice as you can to this woman. But remember, she can use this time to manipulate you. She more than likely will attempt to manipulate you perhaps without even realizing she is doing it. Remember, the "why" of all this will be addressed. Right now we need to get you through the nuts and bolts of this divorce.

Once a woman decides on a divorce and you show the least resistance to the idea, you start to become the enemy. This is a no win situation. If you oppose the divorce and want to make things right and heal your relationship and family, you are perceived on some level as attempting to "control" her, further justifying her desire for the divorce. The more you oppose the divorce, the angrier she will become. She might not express it as anger in a screaming, hissing fit, but she will express her displeasure. If you say fine, go ahead and leave, you are further justifying the divorce in her mind by "proving" that you don't care about her or the marriage. Either way, you can't win.

Instead of fighting the divorce, pursue it. Pursue it with a sense of urgency. If you can, get her to agree to *your* terms for dividing the assets and child custody. If she is in a hurry to divorce you this should be easy. If you think she is stringing you along because she is unsure, *insist* on legalizing the divorce as soon as possible. If she does come back and wants to reconcile at this point, insist on the divorce anyway. Tell her you will take her back, but only on your terms. Later on I will tell you how to deal with future marriages and you need to handle living with her in a marriage the exact same way *if* she comes back.

14

Don't misunderstand me; I am not for divorce at all. But the reality is she has already divorced you emotionally. The longer you wait to legalize her emotions, the longer she has to get the upper hand in divorce court.

Protect Yourself Financially

Things you need to ask your attorney about: Wills, IRAs, stock options and dividends, the house and other property, debt, prenuptial agreements (not as safe as you think), life insurance policies and retirement plans and pensions. You must ensure that your children will be cared for in the event you are incapacitated. Immediately start making copies of all paperwork that has anything to do with the money, her assets, your assets and joint assets and keep them in a safe place. Chances are she will make the attempt to hide some of the assets that are in her name. I know, you think she won't, after all she's hurting over this too. Her attorney isn't.

After consulting your lawyer and if you can legally get away with it, don't wait for the divorce to start dividing the assets. Why? Two reasons: the court will divide things up almost always in her favor *and* you need to let her know right up front that you won't be punked out or wait patiently like some misguided saint willing to take the financial beating she and her lawyer and the divorce court are about to put on you. Get the notions of romantic love that you still have for her out of your head. That love and good will you are having and feeling, secretly hoping for reconciliation won't pay your bills and put food in your mouth once her lawyer is done with you. Consult with your attorney and find out what you *can't* do to financially protect yourself and then go do everything you can do as quickly as possible.

Try not to make it seem like you are hiding assets. No point in it unless you want to get in trouble later. Here are a few ideas to get you started:

Cancel all the credit cards in your name that she has or joint cards and tell her to apply for and get her own. Let her keep one for now if she needs it to facilitate taking care of any children the two of you might have.

Cancel all the joint ATM cards.

Get a cashier's check made out to her and give her enough to open a checking account of her own. Close the joint account and open one of your own.

DO NOT volunteer to move out of the house. Stay in the bedroom, especially if the house and property is in your name and you were the primary breadwinner over the course of the relationship. She wanted the divorce, she wants to leave, let *her* move out, in fact insist on it. You might need to beat her to the punch, no pun intended, with a restraining order in order to do this. Bounce this idea off of your attorney, but DO NOT move out in an attempt to smooth things over with her. It won't work; do everything you can to keep *your* house.

Get her name off the title of at least one of the cars. If possible, have one car put in your name and one car in her name. If both of you are on the loan, pay off one of the cars if you are able as soon as you are able.

Proactively split any joint accounts, dividing things up as fairly as possible on your own. Please don't wait for the court's and your ex's definitions of "fair" to become your reality.

If she has money tied up in stocks and bonds, IRAs, etc. Get a copy of everything. She will hide it if she can, have proof ahead of time.

Start putting hard cash, twenty dollars or so at a time, in an envelope and give it to a friend to keep for you. (Unless of course you think he is the other guy) I recommend you do this at the first sign of trouble or even if things appear to be fine in your relationship. One never knows when a few thousand dollars in cash, tucked away can be of use.

I am not telling you to be a greedy ogre here. I am telling you that her lawyer will be. Protect yourself financially and start doing it **now**. Trust me; there are entire books and websites devoted to helping your wife leave you. Divorce guides for women tell her exactly how to fleece you and how to use the court and social support systems to keep your kids and money away from you.

Protect Yourself Emotionally and Mentally

Don't let her drag the process of the divorce out. If there is another guy in the picture and she isn't sure he is a good enough bet, she will do everything she can to keep you "handy" and make sure you are there to fall back on in case her new prince charming turns out to be a toad. Even if there isn't another man involved, she might be having some serious doubts. It is to her advantage to keep you on a string. Here are a few ways you can tell if she is trying to keep you in the pocket while she assesses the potential relationship with the other man.

First, she will only want a trial separation. Then, you will hear her say things like "I think we need some time and space" or "I love you, but I am not "in love" with you" or "you aren't the same man I fell in love with" and " I feel like we have grown apart". When a woman says any of those things, there is a man on the side or the *hope* of a man on the side, in effect, your replacement. Anything she says that leaves you with the impression that she is not being honest is because she isn't. Make no mistake about it; she is entering the manipulation phase. Manipulation is what she is good at and has been good at since she was a little girl and first learned to interact with boys and men. Eventually she will want to interact with you only in a very, very controlled setting. She might even come over and have sex with you but will refuse to discuss reconciliation. At this point, you are on her little leash while she figures out the rest of the details of her escape.

SHE IS MANIPULATING YOU.

She is your enemy at this point. You might not be her enemy, but she is yours. She will tell any of your friends or hers, the family, etc. that they ought not to give you false hope, while she, in ways subtle and overt, does give you that false hope. She has to give that little glimmer of "I might be home again" hope if she is going to continue to manipulate you and control the situation to her advantage.

Break contact with her immediately.

Offer to call her about child care issues once a week. I recommend e-mail if at all possible. Do not ask where she is, what she is doing or who she is doing it with. She will lie to you and/or get angry because you are trying to control her. Of course, her justification for lying should the truth ever come out is that she was trying to "protect" you. She will try to convince everyone that she didn't want to hurt you. What a crock!!! What a lie!!! If she loved you that much, she would be willing to work things out in order to keep the family together. Genuine love is utterly honest, tactful and kind perhaps, but always honest.

Do not invite her over for dinner, ask to have lunch with her, and offer to fix anything at her new place or anything else. Avoid contact with her at all costs. I know this is hard. You just want to "know". To be honest, it doesn't matter. The more you are around her; the more hurt it will cause you in the long run. Handle legal and financial matters through your attorney and handle childcare issues with a short phone call of e-mail. Do NOT let her engage you in conversation about anything else.

Start to ignore her immediately.

Don't write letters, beg her to come home or send flowers. You are wasting your time and money. Some online "get your wife back" books and relationship gurus tell you to ignore her in order to manipulate her into coming back home. I am telling you to do this because the marriage is over and the sooner you start ignoring her, the sooner you stop being manipulated. This hurts, I know. The unanswered questions are driving you crazy. In order to start healing, and to protect yourself emotionally and mentally, you need as much as is possible to totally cut her out of your life. If there are no children involved and few if any marital assets, get away from her a soon as you possibly can. Maintaining your sanity and emotional balance are paramount if you want to avoid getting manipulated into signing away your life and children. I will explain the psychology behind all of this in a later section, right now you need to take control of your part of this situation and draw a clean and clear line in the sand so to speak. She is on one side and you are on the other. Any attempt on your part to cross this line and reason with, express your love for or woo back the wife is perceived by her as hostility at best and stupidity and gullibility at worst.

You need to go on the offensive. Don't sit around and wait for her to change her mind. Chances are she won't come to her senses for years and perhaps decades and realize she ruined a good thing. Even if she does, it is unlikely she will ever be willing to admit it to you. Immediately take positive control of the situation from a financial and legal stand point at the very least. Once again, this is not to manipulate her into coming home it is to protect you.

Protect Your Children

This is the hard one. The children are the unfortunate victims of the divorce. Even more than the man who is getting left, the children are being torn apart. Mom and Dad are their whole world in most cases. No man who is worth a hoot in Hell wants to see his children hurt and will do anything to protect them. Unfortunately, when a divorce happens, the children are often the first to get ignored. The woman who is leaving seems to be able to convince herself that, "they will be O.K." Statistics say they won't. This is once again the one area, the one and only reason I could see a man being able to justify as a reason to let the wife who has left come back home.

But remember, this is about reality. The reality is she more than likely isn't going to come home. She isn't thinking about what is best for the kids, certainly not what is best for you, she is only thinking about what is best for her at this exact moment.

You must do everything within your power to gain at least 50/50 custody of your children and have as much time with them as possible, regardless of the amount of personal difficulty this places on you. You are the sane and rational half of the equation and your kids need to be influenced by a strong male role model. Your children need you and don't let the traditional notions of mothers being the best parents influence this. When women decided to go out and "be men", when they decided to abandon the traditional gender roles that kept civilization cemented for millennia, they also gave up the role as primary parent. No doubt your children will need and want to spend time with mom, but they must have you be an active part in their lives. Napoleon is credited with saying, "the hand that rocks the cradle rules the world." My friend, when a woman abandons a family for reasons that have to do with "happiness" or a career, they are choosing to take the hand off the cradle. All of the well adjusted, adult children of divorce that I know had strong male influences in their lives. All of the maladjusted adult children of divorce that I know were raised primarily by their mothers without the involvement of a father or other strong male influence.

Chances are your wife, the alleged loving and caring mother of the children, will use those children to get back at you. The angrier she is, the more she blames you for forcing her to have an affair, the more she is unwilling to accept her part in the destruction of your family, the more she will attempt to use the children to get at and manipulate you. She knows you love your kids. She knows the reason you have worked a crappy job and put all of your dreams on hold was for the kids and if she was honest for a minute, for her. That doesn't matter to her. Most of the time, in her immediate pre-divorce mental state, she will attempt to use the kids to manipulate you. She could care less about protecting them or making this transition easy on them. She will do what she can both legally and illegally to keep you from your children. Don't be fooled and manipulated into letting her.

All that said, this is the time when it is absolutely essential that your children, especially your sons, see you acting like a man. I am not talking about a violent aggressive chest beating Neanderthal, I am talking about you being a calm, loving father in their presence. You must not break down and melt and cry in the presence of your children right now. You must make sure they know that Dad has everything under control. If you want to bellow and cry and wallow in the pain, do it alone and away from them.

Right now and really for the rest of their lives, they need to know that Dad loves them more than anything or anyone else. Those children need to be told until they are sick of hearing it how much you love them. They do not need to hear from you what a sorry "whore" or manipulative "bitch" their mother is. You need to practice an extra ordinary amount of patience with them. They are not leaving you; they are not at fault and should never be used to get at the mother.

Every time they arrive or you pick them up ask two and only two questions, first ask then if everything is all right at mom's house. And then ask them if *they* are alright. Don't drag them into the fight; protect them from the situation as much as possible without lying to them. Do not, I repeat, do not ever lie to your children about the situation. If they ask an honest question, give them an honest answer. There is no need to be graphic about adult things, but you must be honest. Children know when Mom and Dad are lying about something important. Even if you think they are fooled and they might be for a little while, they are still going to have memories of this time and memories of the events occurring.

Your job as a Dad is to protect them and provide for them. This means that what you need to set as your number one priority is the welfare, mental, emotion and physical welfare of your children. Get this, you are number two, they are number one. They need someone to make them the priority and that is your job.

Make sure that you continue to celebrate the holidays, birthdays and any other "family" thing you did before your ex left. It might be painful at times, but the children need it to happen. One important thing you can do for them is to create new family traditions; traditions that are exclusive to the new structure. Here are some suggestions: ice cream on a certain day, movie and a pizza on Friday night and a walk in the summer after supper. These new traditions will cement a place in the memories of your children as what they did with you as a family. They will no doubt look back on these memories of that time and think of "home" when they are grown.

All of the above steps will help you get ready for the next step in your journey through this dark time in you life. Once again, cover your rear, and press on with the divorce. I know you think you want her back, but trust me, nine times out of ten, when a man gets to the other side of a divorce he is glad she is gone. If he has been aggressive in protecting himself he will usually only regret that things didn't work out for the sake of his children. You will recover from this and you will be fine.

FIXING YOU

Have you started to get the picture yet? She is gone and hopefully you are starting to accept it as fact. Now what? You are still dying inside. You still hurt like someone is cutting your heart out with a dull, rusty spoon the day before Christmas. The first thing you need to do is fix you and come to terms with what is happening.

The first step to fixing you is accepting that you are partially responsible for what has happened. I don't know why your wife decided you were no longer worthy of her love. There might not even be a real reason. Then again, there might be a very good reason. Are you addicted to something that became more important to you than your family and this has been a wake up call? Be honest with yourself. She no doubt dropped some hints. I am not talking here about some alleged failure on your part to live up to her unfulfilled, idealized notion of romantic love. I am talking about a real dependency or addiction. Is it alcohol? Is it drugs? Did you smack her around and beat the kids? Was your temper and anger out of control? Did you gamble away your family's money? Did you have a woman or two on the side? Were you or are you just a fat, lazy slob? A no good bum?

Unless you can find a woman that finds your addiction and vice attractive, you will find yourself in the exact same position a few years if you get remarried or you will end up old, ugly, poor and alone. If you do stumble across a woman who is looking for someone to be co-dependent with and she finds your addiction attractive, do you really want to have her along while you try and rebuild your life?

Plain and simple, you need to fix you. No doubt you recognize what the problem is now that she has gone. The fact remains that she is gone and she isn't coming back no matter how much you reform. You still need to *take 100% responsibility for your part in the disintegration of the marriage.* Chances are she isn't giving you another shot. In her mind, she has already given you chance after chance to change and she is convinced that you never will. Don't let this affect your decision to get rid of your bad habits and vices. If what she wanted you to change about you wasn't a genuine character flaw, but was instead an excuse for her to bail, don't worry about it. Most important thing about anything she *says* was the reason she left, is for you to examine what she said, be honest with yourself, and fix it if you need to.

Go look in the proverbial mirror and take an inventory. Look long and hard at your life. Decide what, if anything, you need to change and set to work fixing it. This might mean you need to get professional help. If so, do it. This might mean you need to listen to your friends and ask them to be brutally honest with you. If they are your friends, they will be. If your best friend tells you that you have a problem with booze, drugs or anything else, you DO. If your best friend is part of the problem, get rid of your friend. This is *your* life, the only one you get before they throw you in a hole and kick dirt on you. If you screwed up the marriage in some real and tangible way, admit it to yourself, maybe tell her you are sorry for it and move on without her. If you do apologize to her for messing up your half of the relationship, don't expect much of a reaction from her and certainly don't think about apologizing in order to win her back. It more than likely won't work.

Chances are you will be the only one to do this self assessment. Most women don't. Most women who are left seldom if ever look in the mirror and acknowledge that their husband left them for something that might be their fault. When a man leaves a relationship, women usually place 100% of the blame on the man and when the woman leaves, women usually place 100% of the blame on the man. Don't worry about your soon to be ex-wife fixing her life. Don't give in to the temptation to blame her for your problems or addictions.

If you are really messed up, fixing you will take some time. Very few people just stop being addicted to something overnight. That's why it is called addiction. That is why, once again, you might need some professional help. Please, for your sake and the sake of the children, who now more than ever need Dad to be a whole person, get help. If you read this whole book, apply everything else and miss this, you are missing the most important part.

Getting your life Together

When a divorce happens, for the one who did not initiate the divorce, it is as if someone has died. Suicide is 4 times higher for divorced white men as it is for their married counterparts. FACT: Divorce now ranks as the # 1 factor linked with suicide.[1] When a man reaches a certain point in his life, he becomes what I call settled. He usually has a job, can provide for a family and generally has reached a state of satisfaction and CONTENTMENT with his life. Even if things aren't perfect between he and his wife, he has adjusted and can maintain the status quo. All of a sudden, seemingly without warning, she leaves. If there were those wonderfully subtle signs that she was on her way out, we don't pick up on them. We aren't wired that way. We men don't do subtle that well. She will tell you later, if she ever does, that she tried, but in true female meme fashion, she tried her way, the woman way and not in a way that we could readily recognize. This might not be fair, but it is reality. Usually by the time we recognize it, it is too late, she's gone and the man is left reeling.

Now we have to figure out how to live without her around. This can be difficult for men since we tend to break a relationship up into who is responsible for what. Men figure everyone in the relationship, much like a sports team, has a role, a position on the field. We naturally expect everyone to play their role. Modern women don't think that way, the female/feminist meme, which I will discuss later has so deeply embedded itself into our culture that now a relationship is more often about what is fair than what is reality. Wonder why every kid now gets a trophy for playing little league base ball or soccer even if they suck at it? It is the female "fairness" meme run amok. Now that the one who filled the wife position on the team is gone, you will have to learn to play both roles. This can be depressing for some men but it can be done and done well. Women for decades have said that anything men can do women can do as well or better. What a crock!! Do

---

[1] . Brinig, Margaret; Douglas W. Allen (2000). "These Boots Are Made for Walking: Why Most Divorce Filers are Women". *American Law and Economics Review* 2 (1): 126-129.

you see many women on a hot roof on in August? Women like to make us think we need them to take care of our daily lives, cooking, cleaning etc. but the truth of the matter is we don't.

Let's get into the nuts and bolts of how to survive without her.

Don't Kill yourself

I mentioned the suicide statistics for divorced men earlier. These statistics are sad but true. Here is what the Father's for Life website says on the subject:

. . . a divorced father is ten times more likely to commit suicide than a divorced mother, and three times more likely to commit suicide than a married father.[2]

According to Los Angeles divorce consultant Jayne Major:

"Divorced men are often devastated by the loss of their children. It's a little known fact that in the United States men initiate only a small number of the divorces involving children. Most of the men I deal with never saw their divorces coming, and they are often treated very unfairly by the family courts."

According to Sociology Professor Augustine Kposow of the University of California at Riverside, "The link between men and their children is often severed because the woman is usually awarded custody. A man may not get to see his children, even with visitation rights. As far as the man is concerned, he has lost his marriage and lost his children and that can lead to depression and suicide."[3]

I put this section under getting one's life together because I am not just talking about getting a gun or a rope and doing yourself in. I am also talking about letting yourself go physically which is a form of slow prolonged suicide. When the kids are around it is easy to cook a good, well balanced nutritional meal. It is relatively easy to go find things to do with them, swimming at the Y, going to the park, etc. It is not so easy to motivate yourself to do these

---

[2] . National Institute for Health Care Research at 800-580-NIHR. NIHR, 6110 Executive Boulevard, Suite 908, Rockville, Maryland 20852

[3] Walter Schneider , *USA Suicide Deaths 1979 to 1996.*
http://fathersforlife.org/suicides/US_suicide_deaths.htm

things when you are suddenly alone. Right now, in the first months and couple of years after a divorce, it is easy to let yourself slip into a state of depression that ends up with half empty pizza boxes and beer cans scattered around a chair or couch in front of the television. Don't let this happen to you. Think about what life was like before the marriage. Were you active? Did you eat well balanced meals and exercise regularly? No? Well no time like the present to start. Do not let yourself go physically. The stress of divorce can take years off your life. Don't expedite the process any further. Before my divorce I might have had two grey hairs, now well, there are a few more. Go to the gym or take up running. Get yourself in shape.

Getting divorced stacks the deck against you as far as health issues go, why add fuel to the fire by throwing in the towel and giving up emotionally, mentally and physically? You can't, you don't have that option for the sake of your children or yourself.

Here are some more interesting statistics concerning the health of men who have been divorced:

Non-smoking, divorced men have almost the same death rate from cancer as married men who smoke 1 pack or more per day.

Nearly every type of terminal cancer strikes divorced individuals of either sex at higher rates.

Early death from both cardiovascular disease and stroke doubles for divorced men compared to married men.

In a 1990 study of 16 developed countries, unmarried men were twice as likely to die at a younger age as married men. For divorced men, risks were sometimes *10 times* greater than for a married person the same age.

Premature death due to pneumonia for divorced men is more than 7 times that of their married counterparts.

Divorced and separated persons experience acute conditions such as infectious diseases, parasitic diseases, respiratory illnesses, digestive illnesses and severe injuries at higher rates than those who are married.

Heart disease, rheumatoid arthritis and osteoarthritis occur in higher rates in the formerly married. (2)

The deck is stacked against you when it comes to your health. You MUST take steps to beat the statistics. I know, you are depressed and going through an emotional Hell, but in order to get yourself out of this, before it becomes habitual, you need to start taking care of you and your health.

If you *are* considering ending your life, **DON'T** !!!! Before you met your now departed wife, did you think things were so bad that you were willing to end your life? Of course you didn't. You might have struggled with depression or had a suicidal thought over something else but you didn't consider killing yourself over someone you hadn't yet met. Why would you consider it now? It is understandable that the grief and hurt can overwhelm your emotional capability to deal with being left and abandoned by the one you love. When that happens get help. Call a suicide hotline and talk to someone who is trained to help you put things in perspective. Trust me on this, that overwhelming pain will eventually subside. It WILL go away. You will get past this.

If you are finding yourself stuck in a state of grief and depression, get help. A lot of churches now have divorce recovery classes and workshops. Online support groups exist as well. Talk this out with other people who have been through this and made it to the other side. I know you want to withdraw and retreat but talk it out with others who can relate until you are sick of talking about it.

Killing yourself will only prove that the wife was right to leave you. Threatening suicide won't do anything to bring her back either. It will make her despise you even more than she does right now. I recommend at a minimum, getting any guns you have in your house out. Let a friend hold onto them for awhile. This will lessen your chances of doing something impulsive under the influence of drugs or alcohol and it might help protect you legally at some point. (Awfully hard to threaten someone with a gun no longer in your possession.)

Here is some more information and statistics on suicide and divorce from the Suicide Info website:

"One recent study by the National Institute for Healthcare Research in Rockville, MD indicates that divorced people are three times as likely to commit suicide as people who are married. The Institute says that divorce now ranks as the number one factor linked with suicide rates in major U.S. cities, ranking above all other physical, financial, and psychological factors.

A study of 13 European countries by the regional European office of the World Health Organization found that divorce was the only factor linked with suicide in every one of the 13 countries. The study showed that factors like poverty, unemployment, and disability were associated with divorce in some of the countries but that disruption of the family was the only factor linked with suicide in all 13.

Anecdotally, the coroner of Butler County, Ohio told UPI in the late 80's that he thought the high rate of suicide in that area was traceable to men's inability to cope with divorce. Dr. Richard Burkhardt said he thought women were more likely to feel needed after divorce because they needed to take care of children. But men, he said, felt cut off from their role as head of the household and felt they had no reason to live."

Do I need to make the point that your suicide will hurt your children more than you can imagine? Those innocents are already suffering from the destruction of the family unit, the place that was supposed to be a safe haven for them. The fact that your wife has decided her "happiness", affair or career is more important than her children says a lot about how focused she is going to be on the children. They need now more than ever a living breathing father, not a cold buried corpse.

If your wife wants to leave, let her, but don't hand her a silver bullet to help the court decide to keep your kids from you in case your suicide attempt fails. If your ex decides to keep those children from you and the courts help her,

28

there is nothing you can do about it. Be the best dad you can as often as you can. One day, those children will grow up. If she has started poisoning their minds against you, there is not much you can do about it. Once again, one day they will be old enough to make their own choices. When that day comes, you can hope to undo the damage and get to know them the way a father should, but you can only do that if you are alive.

Once more, no woman on the planet is worth taking your own life over. They just aren't. I know you are wondering how I can say this when you are in such overwhelming pain. I can say it because I have lived through what you are experiencing and I came out the other side. I know the crippling pain, the thoughts of escape. I will tell you now, on the other side of the hurt, no pain in the world is worth missing watching kids grow up and being there for them. Your children need you to be here. Even if the court and the ex have severely limited the amount of time you get to spend with the kids, they still need you to be here for them as much as is possible.

Drugs and Alcohol

I am going to ask you to do something for me even if you only drink alcohol socially and have never had a problem with it before. Stop drinking for a while. That's right, stop. Get the stuff out of your house. We all know that alcohol lowers inhibitions. The control over your own life you are trying so hard to maintain and perhaps establish needs a break from the bottle. Jim and Jack won't bring her back. Do I really need to get into illegal drugs? Once again, you just lost your wife; do you want to risk loosing *everything* else in order to dull the pain?

Don't run from the pain, embrace it. That's right, embrace it. I don't know if you ever saw the old Trek movie about Spock's half brother Sybok, Star Trek V: The Final Frontier. In the movie Sybok pulls some kind of Vulcan mind meld trick and "takes away" people's emotional hurt and trauma. He tries it on Captain Kirk and Kirk says to him, "Leave me alone, I don't want you to take away my pain, I need my pain, it has made me who I am, it makes me strong." Kind of a corny, geeky explanation, but it applies. We apply the no pain no gain philosophy to physical training, apply it to your emotional and mental training for life without her as well.

Set your House in Order

I hope you tried or are trying to keep the house. If you didn't and find yourself in an apartment or a rented room somewhere this part will be easy. Now is the time to get rid of a bunch of junk you have accumulated over the years of married life. Most men I know don't need much in the way of "stuff". Think about how much stuff you had when you were single. Some furniture, some clothes, some hobby and sports related stuff and a few tools, maybe a few books if you were a reader and just enough in the way of pots and pans to heat up a can of ravioli and fry a burger. Look around the house now. Crap everywhere. Why do you have all this stuff? Your wife wanted most of it. Now is the time to get rid of all the excess. Those shirts you hated but she liked? Get rid of them. The stupid knick knacks and collectibles she had to have everywhere sucking in all the dust in the State? Yup, get rid of them. Have a garage sale and pocket the cash or start a savings account which you will no doubt need in a few months.

If she cleaned out the house for you that is good. It can be shocking at first to come home to a big empty house. Let her have the crap. Trust me, in the long run this will work out better for you.

I know you will be tempted to burn the entire stack of tear stained pictures you have of her and shred all the letters you wrote her. If you have children I recommend you not do this. Take all the pictures and love letters and anything else that reminds you of happier times with your ex wife, put them in a box, tape it up very well and save it for your children. They will deserve to have access to the good part of the history between you and your wife. Your ex has pretty much rewritten the history of the two of you. In her mind it was all bad and she can't remember the good times. Maybe someday, one of your kids will let her look at the memories you examined one last time and symbolically put in a box. If you don't have children with her, build a big fire and toast the stuff.

Plan for financial recovery

It usually takes a year of hard work to recover from two years of marriage. In other words, if you were married for ten years, it will take five years or so to recover financially. Unless you have or had plenty of disposable income, you are going to need to plan on tightening up the budget. Do this before the divorce is final so when the big child support payment is slapped on you there will be a little reserve. I recommend that you sit down and add up the total amount of child support you will pay over the course of your children's lives, add a few thousand dollars per year and that amount will be how much money you will need to make up.

If your wife worked and contributed to the income of the family you will need to adjust for that as well. It might seem like the screwing you are going to get, the one you didn't ask for, is extreme and more often than not it is. Don't panic. Men don't really need that much to get by on. Think about it for a minute, what amount of "stuff" in your house did you not need when you bought it? Who wanted that stuff? The *mater*, the maternal materialist of the house wanted it, took part of your money and spent it on junk, "niceties". You don't need all that stuff to have a normal productive male oriented life. You don't need ten kitchen knives, you need two. You don't need fifty matching towels; you need maybe ten that will work well enough to dry you off. You don't need to eat out all the time, maybe once or twice a week.

You might want to take on a second part time job in order to make up the deficit for a while. A few nights a week might do it. If you have a hobby that can put some extra cash in your pocket, exploit it. At the very least, you will avoid sitting around the house and wallowing in grief. Empty time, time spent with nothing to think about but her is an enemy right now.

I can't stress this notion of learning to live frugally for a while enough. When I was a medic many years ago in the 82nd Airborne Division, we could go for weeks with what was on our backs, carried in our rucksacks. I am not suggesting that you sell everything and go live like a bum under the bridge. I am suggesting that you plan for the next few years, until you recover from the financial rape of divorce, to live frugally. It will do your spirit and soul good to unlearn the female meme of materialism that you learned while you were married. Like it or not, you are going to be forced to out of necessity, embracing it makes it easier.

Plan for emotional recovery

Divorce is emotionally draining. You were accustomed to getting what you considered to be love from your wife. Even if it was a slight dose grudgingly and selfishly administered it was there nonetheless. Now it is gone. The love has been replaced by rejection which only adds to the deficit. There are several responses to this new emptiness that are destructive in the long run. Don't try to fill that emptiness with more trash. I want to discuss some of these with you but this list of mine is by no means exhaustive.

I know you will be tempted to, but don't fall in hate with your ex. It is easy to let the love you had turn into hatred and contempt for the woman who destroyed your family. Don't do it. Having lived single for awhile and having adjusted to it, I sometimes want to send my ex a thank you card. Don't hate your ex, pity her if anything for buying into the big lie, but don't hate her. Hate is like a poison to the soul. It will shorten your life and destroy you. Jesus said if you hate someone in your heart, you might as well murder them. The woman who walked out is not *worthy* of your hate or contempt. All she is now is the mother of your children if that. If you have to hate, save it for something big like the social forces that destroyed your marriage in the first place. (No, I haven't forgotten the "why")

Closely linked to hate is anger. I know that you are mad and you have somewhat of a right to be. Anger is a destroyer. Unbridled anger is going to make you say and do things that could be detrimental to getting your life back on track. Anger makes you want to go find the other guy and put a .45 slug in him. Anger makes you want to shoot the idiotic "family" court judge after he slams the gavel down and rips your kids away from you and ruins you financially. Anger makes you want to pop your ex in the mouth when she starts brainwashing your children and denying you visitation rights. Anger is your enemy right now, fight the urge to give in to it.

When I was a D.I. in the Army I saw young men get angry quite often. My advice to them is the same to you take that anger and channel it into something else. Emotions have power; they are a kind of psychic energy. Use the anger to fuel something other than an action that will be destructive. Bite your tongue, remove yourself from the situation and refuse to give in to it. Go work out, go for a run, borrow your gun back from your buddy and go to the range but don't express the anger you feel towards your wife and her cronies at the coffee shop and courthouse.

Don't go out looking for a replacement wife right away, if ever. The social forces that led to your "unhappy" wife leaving have affected every woman in our society. I know you are hurting and lonely right now. Women can sense this loneliness in you. Some will sense that loneliness and avoid you because of it. Some will sense that loneliness and try to exploit it for their own purposes, either financially or emotionally. I discuss women in general and the kind of women to avoid in Appendix B, but for right now, take special note of this type woman. Avoid these emotional vampires by not looking for love and affection right now. You need to understand that another woman can't fill the emptiness because she is a different woman than the one you had. Any love you give to a woman right now won't be real love for her, but love for the wife that walked out. Giving that love to another woman isn't fair to you and it isn't fair to the other woman.

Learn for now to live with all the pain and hurt and aloneness. It will go away eventually. The trick is to control the emotions. I don't want to sound like

32

some whacky New Age guru, but you are facing a lack of emotional energy right now. Sometimes when men are faced with this deficit of love we withdraw, it might have happened in your marriage, you weren't getting the love and affection you needed so you withdrew, and all the while the ex was demanding that you feed her. There is a good chance that you have decided that you will just be alone for the long haul. That is OK for now, but make sure you don't distance yourself from the other relationships in your life, especially from your children. Once again, they need to know that you love them fiercely, but **without** using them as emotional surrogates to replace your wife.

Depression can cripple you. If you are spending hours alone, obsessing over your own grief, get some help. Sometimes the depression becomes clinical. Once again get help. As a man, do everything you can on your own to beat this emotional and mental malaise, but if your own devices and attempts to beat depression fail, go get help.

Give yourself time to grieve. If you were one of those whose divorce caught him off guard, this might take some time. If things were bad between you and your soon to be ex wife, the process might not take that long at all. In any event, divorce is like a death of the other person in your life. The difference in becoming a widow and a divorcee is that when someone dies, there is a closure of sorts. When someone dies, it is as if the universe gives you permission to move on. Just like when a man loses his wife to the Reaper, a divorced man needs time to grieve. Let the tears come. At some point though, you have to get up and get on with your life. Only you can know when it is time to stop grieving. I would say this; give yourself a set amount of time, a few months, a year, whatever and then get on with living. Life will go on no matter how sad you are about all of this.

You might regret things said and unsaid when someone dies, but there is simply nothing that can be done. When a couple splits up, quite often the questions are still there, and so is the one who is no longer a part of your life. The reality is, if she left, she has nothing else to say.

Plan for mental recovery

There is no doubt that the divorce you are going through is taking a mental toll on you. Your mind is racing with thoughts of your wife with another man, with the big and seemingly unanswerable question of "why" this is happening and maybe a dozen other things. As I have promised you, the why of your wife's leaving you will be answered shortly. In this section I want to address mitigating the mental impact this divorce is having on you.

If you were in a relationship with a typical Western female, your mind has been tampered with. You have been mentally abused. Think back again to the days before puberty hit and the sexual urge pounded you like a sledge hammer, back when it was just you and the guys running and playing all day. Once you hit puberty and became consumed with the need to spread your seed, you started to actually care what women thought about you. You soon began to allow the female way of seeing things to creep into your mind. You did this in order to get sex, plain and simple. Of course if you were smart and could see through the hormonally induced fog you soon realized that women didn't want you to actually understand them, they wanted you to *want* to understand them. Once a man understands how women operate, without regard to his sexual urges, he doesn't put up with much of their silliness or play their games. That is why little boys think girls are yucky and have cooties. Little prepubescent males don't give a rip what a girl thinks because they don't want to screw them.

This mentality of the female has crept into your life. It has tried to kill and tame and shackle the male energy in you. Women hate this energy, women want to tame you, and they need to *feel* in control of you. In order to peacefully coexist with a woman in Western civilization you allowed part of your masculinity to become subordinate to her desires, needs and wants. As long as you were getting your needs met in an equitable fashion this was fine and a good thing. Now that she is gone, you have no need, no reason, to chain the inner male. I am not telling you to go out in the woods with a bunch of other guys and beat on a drum around a camp fire. I am telling you to go fishing and hunting, to join a sports team and enjoy wallowing in the male meme again. Go camping and sleep next to a fire on the ground. It is time to mentally un-emasculate yourself.

Women will usually always set up a double standard for behavior while screaming for fairness if they are allowed to. Look at the American military as an example. Women demand the right to participate and serve, but they don't insist on an equitable Physical Fitness test. Women want you to treat them fairly, but want to retain the ability and the "right' to treat you in whatever way they see fit. You have been mentally assaulted for years with this double standard of "fairness". It is time to do some reprogramming. It is time for you as a man to reassert genuine fairness and parity in the relationships in your life. It is time to abolish emotion as the standard by which reason and logic are measured. It is time to reestablish logic and reason as the litmus tests of emotion instead. Don't allow your soon to be ex or any other woman you deal with in any setting to insist on what she says is "fair". You, as the man insist on genuine, rational fairness.

Start reading books written by genuine men like Hemmingway. Go rent some old vintage black and white Bogart movies. Go rent a few John Wayne pictures. Watch NFL clips from the days of smash mouth football. Wallow in the male for a while. Burn a few JC Penny and Sears catalogues; use the stinking things reeking of the female material meme as targets at the range. Read technical manuals and encyclopedias, anything that doesn't try to tell you how to feel or think like a woman.

Set a New Path

Most married guys I know have occasionally said something to the effect of, "If I wasn't married I'd . . ." Well, here's your chance. Start backwards planning your life. Remember before you got married and started a family? Hopefully you planned it out. Go to college, meet a girl, get married, have kids, raise the kids, work on climbing the career ladder, graduate the kids, and retire. Guess what? You still can do all those things minus the wife. To be honest, now that you are minus the wife, some of the things you wanted to do, but realized you couldn't because of the wife, well, now you can.

Raising the kids will be easier as well. Think about it; were there ever times in your marriage that you came into direct conflict with your wife over how and what to teach the children? No longer will you have to put up with feminine ideas of "fairness" in child rearing. Don't worry, if they spend any time at all with mom, they will get plenty of indoctrination. You now have the opportunity to balance that feminine influence without interference.

This is the most satisfying part of the whole divorce gentlemen. You are once again in control of your own life. I can't tell you how this will work for you as an individual but I can tell you that there is no time like the present to start planning. Once the children are grown and on their own, execute what you have been planning. I have long had the dream of moving to some thirty acre patch of dirt, within driving distance of a decent city, and just living. In my minds eye I can see a small house, maybe a small garden, and some stupid chickens running around the place, who knows. I could never have done this with either of my ex wives in the picture. They wouldn't have tolerated it for a minute. Now this little dream of mine may or may not happen, but I am free to make it happen if I so choose. **YOU** are free to do the same thing. Ain't it cool?

This is all about perspective. We are free to sit around and mope and cry about our exes or soon to be exes. We are free to drown in grief and pity over the love we lost. We are as equally free to get up, dust ourselves off and get on with our lives.

I will share yet another Drill Sergeant story with you. Seems like every cycle of training, some young man would come into my office heart broken over how his fiancé or girlfriend had sent him a Dear John letter. I would gather all the men into the open bay where they lived and tell them that if they get a letter like this from a woman to send her a thank you note. If a woman is so sorry as to wait until her boyfriend goes off to a high stress situation like basic training to tell him she is breaking up with him, she is a sorry excuse for a girlfriend, a disaster as a future wife and he is better off without her. I told them that a woman who couldn't handle their being gone for a few months of training would no way in Hell be able to handle them shipping off to a war. If the man had a wife who wrote him a Dear John letter I sent him to the Chaplain.

Perspective gentlemen, perspective. You are free to look at this divorce as the end of your life or you can look at it as the beginning. Sure, it is going to be difficult, and so what? Greatness is born from adversity. The great ones never took the easy path. The great ones never curled up in a little ball, stuck their thumbs in their mouths and withered away. A part of you is dying, it is time to start living again. You have the rest of your life ahead of you, make it count. Make it count because a lot of people are depending on you. There are mountains to climb, stuff to invent, patients to heal, court cases to win, businesses to start and women to meet.

OTHER THINGS TO DEAL WITH

There are a few other situations I want to address. These things may or may not exist in your case. If they don't, fine read it and use it later if you need to.

Her Lover

Yup, inevitably it happens. You find out about the other guy. Best advice, **ignore him. He's an idiot.** He is taking in, having an affair or whatever with a woman who is leaving her family. No doubt they are having sex and were having sex long before you found out about him or suspected anything like this was going on. If he is married and leaving one woman for another he is being a double idiot. (If you have stumbled across this book and are doing that same thing, you are being an idiot. Sorry, no matter how bad your ex was, chances are you are replacing her with a woman quite similar to or exactly like the one you are leaving her for.)

Don't go to this moron and confront him or threaten him. He is going to tell your ex, giving her more justification for doing what she is doing. The idea here is that your soon to be ex needs to take full responsibility for what she has done and is doing. Anytime you make a scene of any type, you are only giving her more opportunity and ammunition to blame **you** for her being a covenant breaker and a cheater. I know he needs a good old fashioned ass whipping, let God or Karma or the universe give it to him, just not you..

Just ignore him. Chances are he is taking advantage of the free sex your wife who vowed to be faithful to you, who vowed to give her body only to you, is providing. She won't see this, she won't get it so don't waste your time trying to convince her. She *wants* to believe that even though he is helping break up a family, that somehow, he has only noble intentions. He is treating her like a whore for all practical purposes. There is nothing you can do about this, nothing.

There is an old saying, "The best thing you can do for the man who steals your wife is to let him". Whatever issues your ex had that she blamed on you will resurface. I have heard from scores of men who told me the same thing. At some point a few years after the divorce, the kids would tell them about the troubles Mom was having with your replacement. She might even call you up herself and tell you. It is the same story as your marriage but with a different man playing the "husband" role. A good number of these men have told me that at some point the ex asked to come back. But by then they had moved on and it was too late.

Do draw the line at this idiot coming in and trying to replace you as the father of your children. If your ex is encouraging this, do whatever you can to counter this without making a scene. Have a talk with your kids about this situation if they are old enough. Explain to them that they don't have to call the guy "dad" and indeed they shouldn't. Make sure they know that if he crosses the line with them in any way that they are to tell you immediately. Then take legal action if you feel it is warranted.

I know you want to know what made her decide to trade you in for the other guy. I know what she is telling you. She is telling you that he "understands her" or he treats her better, etc. She has convinced herself of what a great guy he is. Chances are she is the only one in the world with intimate knowledge of the details that believes he is a great guy. Great guys, good men, don't mess up other people's marriages. No doubt there are some people who are giving this little romance an approving nod, but the average person, with no dog in the hunt would say he is a bad man of low moral character.

Here's what happened: The two of you were going along living life, perhaps raising children, and had fallen into something of a rut. There were some problems, but the two of you had made adjustments to live with your differences. Now, according to her reasoning, you aren't the same romantic, obedient puppy she had fallen "in love" with and gotten married to. You became boring and unappreciative of her contribution to the "relationship". So she starts a process of triangulation. Triangulation is taking two known points and finding another as of yet unknown point. The two of you are the known points so to speak and he or the hope of a "he" as portrayed in the mass media and in romance novels is the unknown point.

She meets this new guy and gets those butterflies in her stomach. The butterflies are what we call being "in love". We all get them, but most people who are mature recognize infatuation for what it is. Your soon to be ex hasn't. She might on some level, but it can't trump the romantic love and "happiness" she has been told she "deserves" by society. She starts a compare and contrast campaign. Mentally and emotionally she starts to compare the two of you. Guess what? Thanks to her current emotional state, you lose. Never mind that you have been working like a dog for years to make a good living and provide for your family, never mind that you never cheated on her, never mind that the two of you had children together or took a vow of "until death do us part" together. Her unhappiness with the relationship the two of you have is compared to the new "perfect" man and an unknown future relationship with him, one that in her mind consists of eternal happiness and bliss. Why? Because she has decided that he is "better" than you. So, in due time she convinces herself that not only he is more romantic, more kind, smarter, etc., but that YOU are "bad". After she makes this mental leap, the criticism starts. You are constantly bombarded with criticism and God forbid if she is just by nature a critical person and has been critical of you for years already.

Well, if you are "bad", according to all her friends in miserable marriages or divorced themselves she shouldn't be expected to stay with you. If you are "bad", how can she continue to love you? If you are a living breathing reminder of how "great" and wonderful the object of her infatuation and lust is, why should she stay with YOU? That's when you will hear things like, "I need time and space" or "I love you, but I am not in love with you."

From this point on, she will begin to rewrite her mental history of the marriage. This might happen whether or not there is another guy in the picture. All of the good times and happiness you shared will be de-emphasized. All of the bad times, arguments and anytime you did or said something that "hurt" her will become the only valid memories of the relationship she is ending. It doesn't matter that you might remember the same marriage a bit differently; her reality is the only one that matters at this point. In her reality you are evil, the relationship was empty, hollow and totally miserable and the other guy is her brand new, fresh out of the box, with styrofoam packing falling off, Prince Charming.

That's the deal with the "other man" and once again, there is nothing you can do about it. In fact, the more you try to do, the worse it makes the situation. Once again, ignore him. Don't worry, why she is behaving this way will be explained as promised.

The In-laws

The In-laws will inevitably take her side. Bet on it. They might have even been encouraging her behavior. They might have been bad mouthing you for years behind your back or in front of you. You have to be cordial to the grandparents for the sake of the kids, but you don't have to continue to feel obligated to them in any way. You might have a good relationship with them and they might still want you to be a part of their family. All this is fine, but once again, you aren't obligated to them in any way.

Avoid talking to them about the situation at all if possible. Eventually they will choose her over you. They are her parents; they are supposed to take her side in things. Remember this too, if she was close at all to her parents, anything you tell her parents will get back to her. They should be considered co-conspirators especially until the divorce legalities are settled and final.

Her friends

They are not on your side in this. Never ever ask them anything and never ever tell them anything you don't want your ex wife to know. They will ignore the things that she is doing that scream she is having an affair. They might help her lie about it. If she is not having an affair, they will still encourage and support her in her "decision". That is why they are her friends. Any woman who doesn't support her decision to bail on the marriage will shortly cease to be her friend.

Her friends might even be as much a part of the problem as the other guy if there is one. They will no doubt encourage her delusional thinking and engage in it with her. Women who aren't having problems with their own marriages will not approve of her actions or will remain neutral. The women who are in her circle of friends that are in crappy marriages or who have been married multiple times will more often than not support this decision of hers whole heartedly.

One of her friends might decide to try and get you to have sex with her. She could be doing this for any number of reasons. Be very, very wary of any of your soon to be exes' friends who come on to you. She wants you for herself, she is helping her friend, your wife, set you up for later or she is trying to get back at your ex for something, maybe for sleeping with her husband.

DO NOT TRUST HER FRIENDS, Period, ever.

SEX

Sex, the universal solvent, as needful to good emotional and mental health as anything ever invented. Perhaps you weren't getting any of it before the disintegration of the marriage began. Perhaps you were and she abruptly cut you off once she decided she would eventually leave you. Perhaps she decided to put it on you good and proper right before she left. What ever your situation, you need to be careful about the stuff during and right after a divorce. Don't go crazy and waste a great deal of time looking to get laid. You aren't ready. I know you could, but chances are, unless you are going to do the dangerous one night stand thing (STD) with a woman you meet in a bar, you aren't emotionally ready to have sex yet. You hopefully have been doing it with the same woman for all the years of your marriage. In most cases, what a man going through a divorce wants is not the raw sex, but the intimacy he once had with his wife. Sorry buddy, she's not giving it to you anymore because she no longer loves you. Good lesson here for married guys who are reading this. If your wife isn't giving it up, there is a problem in your relationship besides her lack of interest in sexual intimacy.

Women mentally and emotionally connect sex with two things and two things only, love and money. You can meet women who will have sex with you for the sake of just having sex. They do exist. But at some point in the relationship they will want to establish, indeed must establish, an emotional connection. It is in the nature of the gender. Don't think you can have sex with a woman more than a few times before she wants there to be a relationship to go along with the sex. They are wired that way. The other thing women associate with sex is money. Prostitution is not called the world's oldest profession for nothing. If you are having sex with a woman who doesn't want a relationship with you, she will eventually want something of material value from you. If you don't mind exchanging goods and services for sex, knock yourself out.

The danger of having sex with a woman right after your divorce is that you are more than likely still emotionally connected to your wife. If you are having sex with a woman during this period you had better be prepared to give her either a relationship or material goods. I won't preach to you about the morality of sex. That is up to you to figure out. If you are religious, you more than likely have some principles associated with sex outside of marriage. I would suggest those who are religious follow those moral precepts outlined by your faith and Scripture. For those who have no particular objection to sex outside marriage, I would urge you to tread lightly and not go out looking for it. You might get lucky, but at the end of the night, you will still feel empty and alone until you recover emotionally from the divorce.

41

You might be thinking, "Yeah, right, I'll never have sex again." Hmmm, let's see, you had sex with your wife right? At least in the early stages of the relationship and hopefully at least *some* sex went on during the marriage. If you were sexually active before your marriage, why do you think this is the end of your sex life? The ONLY reason I could think of would be for religious reasons. There are volumes written on how to attract a woman regardless of income and physical appearance. Once the smoke clears, pick up some of the stuff written and get busy!!!!!

The Urge to Remarry or Find another Woman

Right now you are alone and lonely. Even if you were in a less than stellar relationship, the fact remains that you actually had a relationship. Chances are you loved the woman who has walked away. You no doubt wanted to love her but could never figure out quite how she needed or wanted to be loved. Perhaps you had given up and assumed that everything was fine. Now, for the first time in years you are facing life alone. It sucks to be there. But let me tell you this, if you are over thirty five and have had all of your children, there is nothing a woman can offer you that you really need except sex. Forget all the love and companionship stuff. If you are living in Western Civilization there is a good chance your ideas on love, marriage and relationships with women are screwed up anyway.

I will explain later why Romantic Love is a myth. Right now I want to address the nuts and bolts part of why you don't actually need a woman in your life, as a wife anyway.

You have had children. What good is a woman to you in any real, practical sense if you have already met the biologic requirement to perpetuate the species? The modern American woman is a terrible cook, hates and often refuses to do housework, can't seem to do the simplest of tasks on her own and is usually overweight thanks to not actually having to do much hard manual labor anymore.

Do you need a woman around to help clean the house? They always told you that they worked too and needed help around the house. What a bunch of crap. A 3000 square foot home can be kept clean and neat with one day's work. The laundry included. I know, I give my own house a good cleaning once a week. The yard work and repairs usually take a half a day once a week. She's not too tired, she's either lazy or she has bitten off more than she can chew and needs to prioritize. What do most women do at work exactly that

42

saps them of so much energy? Do they frame houses all day? Do they build bridges? Do they pour cement? Are they working hard to solve difficult engineering and mathematical problems? Are they delivering freight? Are they working under the hood of a car all day turning wrenches? Chances are no. Chances are your ex-wife's job consisted of going to an office somewhere and moving electronic digits around on a computer and shuffling some papers around on a desk and maybe sending a few e-mails and sitting in the all important "meeting". This is not to degrade women and what they do, it is a simple fact that most men have jobs that are physically more demanding than most women.

Do you need a woman to cook for you? No you don't. You can cook nutritious, filling meals like your grandmother cooked for your grandfather with a one hour trip to the grocery a week and a half hour in the kitchen every night if you are cooking for yourself and a little longer when you have the kids. Of course you could always do what the typical America does, you could get take out or shove something from a box, in the microwave and have dinner on the table in a few minutes.

Do you need a woman around to make you feel masculine by opening the pickle jar for her and unclogging the sink and maybe killing the occasional spider or mouse? No, you don't. Instead you can watch an entire ball game without being asked to do something that your grandmother could have done without any assistance what so ever, while she was making real homemade biscuits instead of something from a cardboard tube.

Do you need her around to help you remember to do things her way, when and how she wants them done? I bet a dollar any and everything your wife contributed to the relationship in a practical sense you can manage just fine by yourself. Chances are in time and with a little practice, you will be able to do those things more efficiently and better than she ever did them.

Do you feel the need to go shopping for useless junk once a month or week? If you feel the sudden urge to go to the mall and look for great deals on "stuff" send me an e-mail, you can pick me up a pair of socks while you are there.

The only thing you need a woman for at this point in your life is sex. That's it. Oh wait, I forgot companionship. What was the "companionship" like at your house before she left? Were you taking long walks on the beach and holding hands and sharing the intimate details of your future together or were you sitting in a chair channel surfing every night? Perhaps you were caught up in the soccer mom "I have to take Johnny and Suzy to every stupid thing I can sign them up for to avoid actually parenting" syndrome. Maybe now that your wife is gone you and the kids can actually spend real time together and you can teach them about how life really works without the ex rolling her eyes at you or attempting to undermine your authority as a father. If you are getting divorced, there more than likely wasn't much genuine companionship in your marriage to begin with, at least not towards the end. You are already used to the lack of companionship in a practical sense.

What you are missing so terribly right now from your soon to be ex wife is the *idea* of having a wife around. I know you miss her presence, the small amount of genuine love she was giving you before she walked out perhaps. You aren't really missing all that much. Chances are what you are feeling isn't a genuine loss of *her* companionship so much as the realization that there was and is *no* companionship at all. You have been like a hungry man living next to a bakery. Her leaving has only accentuating what you were already devoid of.

Does the need for companionship exist? Of course it does, but companionship can be had without the cost of another statistically doomed exclusive relationship or marriage. Once you have calmed down some emotionally and have figured out how to live alone. You will find that you have plenty of spare time. You can find companionship by doing things like taking dance lessons, joining a volunteer group, taking a lesson in a group, going back to school or getting involved in a church group. Trust me on this one gentlemen, there are scores of nice women out there who have been duped by a worldview at odds with marriage and they are looking desperately for a man to spend time with. A good many of these women have come to their senses and realized they made a mistake and they are looking for another chance. This doesn't mean that you have to become exclusive with or marry any of them. It does mean that there is a pool of single women for you to do things with and find companionship based on common interests.

If you haven't had children yet or if you want to have some more and want to have the nuclear family, the little house with a sweet wife and a white picket fence, your chances of having that little fantasy come true are slim to none. Society has taught women that your dream is their slavery. If you do find one who wants the same thing, her version of it is not based in the reality of a genuine marriage, but rather the mythology of Romantic Love. There is a way to accomplish this goal without selling your soul. At the end of the book, in Appendix B, I will explain how to do this.

Don't get me wrong. I am not opposed to the nuclear family and the white picket fence. I will tell you that in order to have that, you will need to look long and hard for a woman who will want the same thing for the *rest* of her life. Feminism has taught women that simply being a wife and mother is a bad thing, an oppression of sorts. Women who start out at an early age wanting to be just wives and mothers start getting bored once the kids are in school and since feminism teaches them that marriage is oppression etc. that boredom turns to unhappiness. Once that happens, the white picket fence becomes as desirable as a heart attack and the "unhappy" and "unfulfilled" woman seeks to find that happiness she doesn't have. The cost is usually the end of the marriage.

In order to have that idyllic life, you must find a woman who understands the destructive powers and forces at work in our culture and who will be your ally in keeping those forces from having an impact on your family. They *are* out there but are becoming increasingly difficult to find.

The bottom line is this, you are much better off without the woman in your life that is divorcing you once you have had your children. You have no need for a woman now except for the occasional roll in the hay.

Dating Again

I know that some of the "Get your wife back" books recommend that you go out and start dating again right away. These books recommend that you do this in order to make your wife think that you are going to be fine without her and that she will all of a sudden realize what a desirable man she is loosing and she will want to come scurrying back to you. That might work. I haven't actually seen it work but it might. But look at what you are doing if you choose to do that. You are first and foremost attempting to fake a desire for another woman. If that isn't how you actually feel yet, you are actually using another woman in order to get your wife to come home. Is that what you really want to do? Is that the kind of person you want to be? Women usually "date" in order to find a prospective mate. Try it if you want to but most women worth having won't date a man who is separated, or still married with a divorce pending final dissolution. They are afraid of falling for a man who might go back to his wife. No one wants to get hurt any more than life has already hurt them. If you do date again soon, don't do it in order to get the ex back. In fact, don't do it until you have decided you aren't going to take her back *if* she decides to come home.

Once you do decide to date again, proceed with caution. You might find this hard to believe, but there are women out there who are looking for a guy just like you in your particular situation. These women fall into two categories. In the first group are the ones who have been treated unfairly in love and life and are looking for a good man to have a relationship with. These women won't want you until you are over your ex. These women usually have jobs of their own, clean houses, well behaved children, no anger towards men in general and are emotionally, mentally and physically healthy. In the second group are women who know that you are emotionally vulnerable and partially unavailable. These women don't care; they are desperate to find a man, any man with a job. These women are seeking to find "happiness" and a paycheck. They are miserable, lonely creatures who have walked away from a perfectly good or salvageable marriage and man or have driven a good man off. These women can sometimes be hard to identify. They know exactly what to do and say to capture your attention. A good rule of thumb is to never date women who left their husbands unless he was beating them or abusing the children. Never ever, ever date a woman who left her last husband simply because she wasn't "happy".

Some more women to avoid at this point in your life are the one's who want to help fix your broken heart. There might be a few who will do this for altruistic reasons, but most have an agenda. Most women who want to "help you get over her" are going to be trouble for you in the long run. These women see you as flawed and want to remake you into a man they can control. There are of course women who will sense your vulnerability and loneliness and use that as a quick trip to your pocketbook. Sometimes women like this aren't easy to spot. If the woman you decide to date says she understands where you are emotionally and wants to just stay friends, but expects you to pay for everything, she is a whitewashed gold digger. You get to pay for her supper and trips etc. but she is or will be unwilling to take the relationship to the next level, even when you are eventually ready.

There are a dozen and one lists of "types" of women to avoid when you first start dating. Go and do some research if you are getting back into the dating scene or planning on it any time soon. Please don't misunderstand me. I date on a regular basis, movies, dinner, coffee, whatever. But I am doing so for the right reasons and more importantly, with my eyes wide open. That right reason is simply to enjoy the company of women.

We have covered a lot of simple, common sense stuff. Most of the time the initial stages of being left leave an otherwise normal man emotionally and mentally off balance. I want you to know that other men have been through this and survived. You *will* survive this and you will be better off in the long run if you allow yourself to be better off. You have been hurt. A part of your soul has been cut out, amputated. You must do what all amputees do

46

and you must do it quickly. You must learn to adapt and live with the pain and loss. Eventually that empty part of your soul will start to fill in and heal. No doubt it will take some time. But remember this, the woman who left you was only a part of your life as was your relationship with her. She might have been a big part for many years. That part of your life is over now. Now, you have the rest of your life to live with all the wisdom and knowledge you have thus far acquired. Her leaving has only added to that wisdom. You can, you will and you must go on and get on with your life.

Once you decide to date again, take it slowly. As crazy as this might sound, I recommend using an online dating service at first. If you were married for any length of time and had a heart for your ex wife, being in the "game" again is going to feel a bit odd. This might annoy some people who read this, but most women I dated after meeting them online weren't really good long term relationship material. It might take you awhile to get your confidence up again. Remember, you have learned a lot about women in general from this experience.

THE BIG WHY

Here it is . . . the big **why**. Why did a woman with a good many years invested in a relationship and a marriage walk out the door, leaving behind a man who loved her and only wanted her to make a family with her? Why would she just give up and leave?

There are two distinct forces at work in our culture pulling women almost in half. Both of these forces are the inventions of human beings. Both of these memes exist and are real and prey daily upon the minds of unsuspecting women from the time they can walk. These memes are Feminism and the ideal of Romantic love. Neither of these things exists in nature. We will examine both historically, and I will tell you why your marriage barely stood a chance in the face of two of the greatest intellectual and emotional hoaxes ever perpetrated on the human race. These forces are the mental and emotional manifestation of the memes of Romantic Love and the socialist related construct of Feminism. These two ideas are incompatible and almost mutually exclusive. These two opposing memes are waging a war for supremacy and dominance inside the heart and mind of every woman in Western civilization. A meme is defined as a unit of cultural information that represents a basic idea that can be transferred from one individual to another.

Chances are your wife is a victim of this internal struggle between wanting mythological Romantic love and the external demands of Feminism. She will tell you she left because she wasn't happy, because she didn't feel supported and appreciated and that might be exactly how she actually does feel. She no doubt *feels* completely justified in her decision to leave you. The bigger question is *why* she felt that way in the first place.

Here is the short answer to why your wife and other wives not being beaten and abused, who have all the ingredients required for a long and fulfilling marriage decide to walk away. Romantic love creates the expectation of a false reality by which women measure the men in their lives. Once a man fails to measure up to the myth of Prince Charming, Feminism gives them a false reason and the real ability, via the government, to leave the family unit. This process may take decades to come to its final conclusion. It may take a few years. But it is a process and it is happening and has happened to any woman who is not cognizant of it.

I am not going to turn this into a research paper. I am going to describe Romantic love and Feminism, give a brief history of marriage and then tie it all together. Once you let this information sink in, you will realize that modern marriage as an institution is pretty much useless to men and unless we do something to change the dynamics of relationships between men and women, marriage as we now know it is one of the stupidest things a man can do.

Romantic love

Romantic love according to most historical sources was an invention of French poets and musicians, troubadours, in the late middle ages. This is not to suggest that humans had never acknowledged the state of being "in love" before this time. Before this idea became the definition of what love is supposed to be like, the "in love" state, was never held as a primary reason to marry or enter into a marriage contract. Of course people who loved each other got married, but the reasons for marriage were not limited to this chemical imbalance in the human brain. More often than not the families of the man and woman involved; the parents of the prospective bride and groom, specifically the father of the bride had to approve. If daddy didn't approve, the contract was never entered into. Fast forward to modern America and we find Romance novels, books, magazines, television and movies defining for us what it means when a man loves a woman. That definition and not the definition of love that keeps people together is what has become the reason to marry.

Historians can find no evidence of courtly Romantic love from before about eight hundred years ago. "What about the Bible" you might say, doesn't it talk about love? Sure it does. It even has a story that tells us what a disaster the idea of making Romantic Love a standard for marriage can be. Read the story of Jacob and Rachel. Jacob was instantly smitten over Rachel. It was "love at first sight". Her daddy tricked him and gave her older sister Leah to be his wife after the idiot worked for seven years to get Rachel. A week later, Jacob got Rachel but had to work an additional seven years to pay off daddy. Guess who the best wife was? The ugly older sister, that's who, Jacob's use of Romantic Love as a factor in choosing a wife was stupid. Romantic Love wasn't a standard or requirement for marriage until recently. No doubt men and women loved each other, but there was more at stake in the marriage contract than the chemically induced feeling of euphoria and outright horniness being "in love" produces.

Most Western women who believe a man to be "in love" with them expect certain behaviors that have little to nothing to do with the practical and real matters of a relationship. Men have been brainwashed into sometimes ignoring or at least subordinating the realities of a life time commitment and their own needs to a woman in order to meet the woman's expectation of a proper expression of his "love".

Romantic love is what leads women to want a big wedding in a white dress and a huge chunk of rock on their finger, a wedding that is essentially about *them* What big two or three paycheck gift did they give you when the two of you got engaged? Oh, she kept having sex with you until the wedding was over? Romantic love is the de facto definition of love embraced by women and forced on men in today's society. It is a myth. The kind of prince charming, come sweep me off my feet and rescue me from perpetual loneliness and my current state of unhappiness, love that women seek is an impossible standard. This kind of love teaches women that a man's primary function in life is to serve primarily her emotional needs and secondarily her physical needs. By physical, I don't mean her sexual need, that is usually an after thought to most women who hold fast to notions of Romantic Love. By physical needs I mean the getting of "stuff" for her and to ensure that by the getting of enough stuff, she will have a certain level of security.

Romantic love also means that she is always right. Real love doesn't always say "As you wish." like Wesley in the movie *Princess Bride* That is a fairy tale. But, most women have been conditioned by this notion of love and have chosen to make that the definition of what it means when a man loves them. Consider the movie *Forrest Gump*. As a guy, I like the movie because Forrest was open and honest and true to exactly who he was. The raw nobility of Gump appeals to me as a man. He believes in God, and lives like it. He is a man of his word acting on what he knows to be real and right. He is a genuine friend to his friends.

Look at why the average woman likes the movie; because no matter how badly Jenny treated Forrest, he still loved her. I remember watching women weeping over it and saying that exact thing, "He *loves* her." That kind of love, while pure and admirable, is not a reason to get married. Forrest finally does marry Jenny, but only after she has run around like a whore, become a druggie, contracted AIDS, conceived a child with him that she kept out of his life for six years or so and finally realized she was dying. She didn't want to marry him until she hit the bottom of the barrel. As good a guy as Forrest was in the movie, in real life, he was a chump. Stupid is as stupid does I guess. And Forrest is exactly how women want men to be..... I hope that helps illustrate how one sided a woman's notions of Romantic love are.

Dr. Belle Muschinske, PhD, MFT describes the expectations of romantic love:

Love conquers all. One of the most popular and dangerous, this says love is everything, discounting the need for communication and conflict resolution skill and some matching of interests and values.

Angerless love. If you love me you will not be angry with me, and vice versa. Proper expression of anger is essential in healthy living and loving. Anger is not the opposite of love; indifference is the opposite of both.

Love without conflict. Not only is some conflict unavoidable, its total absence is a far greater danger sign.

Magical knowing. If you love me, you should know what I'm feeling, thinking, & needing. Mind reading is not yet a proven human capability! More likely this is an excuse for claiming to be misunderstood and neglected.

True love should lead to marriage. One of the most popular, yet most ill advised myths derived straight out of Romanticism, this one neglects to warn that there may be some individuals with whom one may be in love, but well advised NOT to marry. During a typical lifespan, there may be several true loves.

Love means never having to say I'm sorry. Wasn't there a book by this title? If so, for heavens sake toss it! This myth takes away all accountability. It merely provides an excuse to be or do whatever one wants regardless of its consequences on others.

If you're even a little attracted to others, love is dying. Truth is, this means you're alive and well. You will probably be attractive to and attracted by many others. Mature love can accept such feelings without acting on them.

The right partner will meet ALL of my needs. No human being can nor should be expected to meet all of their partners needs. Truthfully, no one must have all of his or her needs met to be whole and healthy. The fact is a majority of people has no idea what their needs are.

Good marriages just come naturally. All that this outgrowth of Romanticism does is relieve one of the responsibilities needed for working at the marriage.

Have you heard these things, or variations of these things from you ex wife or other women? Maybe you believe some of this cultural stupidity. Understand where this comes from. Understand that Romantic Love is a myth, an impossible standard that we are expected to live up to and often expect others to live up to.

When a man no longer stirs the modern woman's passions and can no longer live up to the definition of a man "who loves her" according to the definition and expectations of Romantic Love, the woman becomes "unhappy". What is happiness? *Happiness is an emotional response to external stimulus.* When a woman becomes unhappy in or with a relationship, she soon decides that she no longer "loves" the man because according to her definition, the one pounded into her brain by cultural and media representations of Romantic Love, he no longer loves her. Trust me on this one all you men who are wondering why your wives' left you. She is convinced that she no longer loves you because you no longer meet her expectations of Romantic Love. The reality of what genuine love is has been suspended in favor of a puppy dog paws and a rainbow and glitter fantasy.

I am not against love, either genuine love or the state of being "in love". Being in love and loving another can be a grand thing. It can be a wonderful experience. In fact, "in love" is a healthy natural part of a person's initial meeting another and establishing a relationship. The expectations in our culture associated with this condition are the problem. There is a huge difference between happiness and contentment. Happiness comes and goes. If someone wishes to be happy all of the time, they haven't a firm grasp on reality. Contentment is achievable on a steady and consistent basis. Happiness is not.

The arrangement worked quite well for centuries. Men would fall in love with women, women would fall in love with men, and they would decide to get married. Once they entered into the marriage contract, each one of them was expected by society to fulfill certain obligations. The man would be sexually faithful and the woman would grant access to her body on a regular basis, this ensured children and the perpetuation of the species and an extended family unit. The man would go out and find employment or start a business (most often a farm) and the woman would do certain things that freed up the man's time to work for a family instead of just him, more often than not she would handle the domestic duties. This arrangement made sense since she would be carrying the young and providing nourishment via her breasts for the first few years of the child's life.

This arrangement wasn't predicated on you, the man, being the "One" true love of her life. It was predicated on who could and would be the best provider *and* mutual attraction. The families of the potential bride and groom acted as a common sense valve in cases of extreme romantic love and "smitten-ness". This notion of romantic love and your failure to live up to it is why the average woman today acts like a spoiled self centered princess as she is walking out the door. In her mind she is the princess and you were supposed to be the Beast tamed and conquered by the Beauty. You weren't the "one" instead you ended up being like most every other man on the planet. So, in accordance with the notion of Romantic Love, she is out the door to continue her quest for the "one".

The difference between Romantic Love and genuine or mature love is important to understand. Here are some indicators of genuine or mature love:

Genuine love is grounded in reality. Mature people realize that they are going to have to have a relationship in the real world. In the real world problems aren't solved during a half hour or hour long television program. In the real world people are flawed beings who make mistakes. In the real world, men go bald, women "sag" in certain areas and we all get fat. In the real world people have bad days and say and sometimes do things that hurt the ones they love. In the real world, forgiveness is a requirement.

Genuine love grows out of time. Mature love is what is left when the fires of lust and infatuation burn away. In the real world, true love, the kind that lasts doesn't happen overnight and it doesn't end because someone is temporarily "unhappy".

53

Genuine love is mature enough to suffer *at times* for the sake of the object of the love but is not expected to. If two people genuinely love each other in the real world, they sacrifice, without bitterness, for the object of that love. They realize that real life is hard and sometimes the needs of the family unit come ahead of the wants and desires of one person. If a person claims to love another, but refuses to be inconvenienced for that person, or becomes bitter over it, then I suspect what they had was not love in the first place

Genuine love is less tied to emotion and more tied to commitment. The "in love" feeling inevitably goes away. It is a chemical euphoria that lasts at best a few years. After that, the real love is all that's left and sometimes, there is not much. That is why we came up with the idea of a committed monogamous relationship in the first place. I am convinced that two people can make a lifetime go of it after the "in love" stage is over. That takes commitment. It sounds like such a burden, but really it isn't unless one is driven to live in a state of perpetual happiness.

Genuine love is grounded in reality, Romantic Love isn't. In the early days of Courtly and Romantic love, the idea was that the object of that love was unattainable. Fast forward to the rise of the middle class and the idea of unattainable Romantic Love as practiced by the nobility was embraced by the middle class. The wide spread use of printed materials for popular entertainment during the industrial revolution and the notions of romantic love became widespread and seemingly attainable. But Romantic love is still at best a chemical euphoria that fades over time and at worst an artificial construct.

Genuine love is the kind of love that makes men and women stay together even when they fall "out" of love. Genuine love is not predicated on what another does for us or what we do for them but what we agree to do for each other. This type of love realizes that "happiness" is not the litmus test of its loyalty and faithfulness to the other person in the relationship. Mature people realize that they do not have a God given right to be happy all the time once they commit themselves to another person and the creation of a family. As a matter of fact, that commitment ensures periods of unhappiness.

Let me take a minute to add something to the earlier section about surviving your divorce. If you are pinning away after your ex-wife, sending her cards and flowers and letters and generally allowing yourself to be convinced that she was the "one" for you as she is walking out the door, you are helping to perpetuate the myth. She isn't the "one" if she is leaving you.

Unfortunately love, be it deep and genuine or the stuff of invented mythology, and the resulting matrimony comes into conflict with another invented social norm.

Feminism

What is Feminism? By feminism do I mean women asking to be treated with respect and dignity? Nope. By feminism do I mean women asking for equal pay for equal work? Nope. What do I mean when I say Feminism? I'll let the Feminists themselves tell you what I am referring to:

"The end of the institution of marriage is a necessary condition for the liberation of women. Therefore it is important for us to **encourage women to leave their husbands and not to live individually with men**... All of history must be re-written in terms of oppression of women. We must go back to ancient female religions like witchcraft." (*The Declaration of Feminism*, November 1971).

"Since **marriage constitutes slavery for women**, it is clear that the women's movement must concentrate on attacking this institution. Freedom for women cannot be won without the **abolition** of marriage." (Radical feminist leader Sheila Cronan)

"We can't destroy the inequities between men and women until we destroy marriage." – (*Sisterhood Is Powerful*, Robin Morgan (Ed), 1970, p.537.)

"How will the family unit be destroyed? . . . the demand alone will throw the whole ideology of the family into question, so that women can begin establishing a community of work with each other and we can fight collectively. Women will feel freer to leave their husbands and become economically independent, either through a job or welfare."
— *Female Liberation*, by Roxanne Dunbar.

"I believe that women have a capacity for understanding and compassion which man structurally does not have, does not have it because he cannot have it. He's just incapable of it." (former Congress Woman Barbara Jordan)

"I want to see a man beaten to a bloody pulp with a high-heel shoved in his mouth, like an apple in the mouth of a pig☐.... "The traditional flowers of courtship are the traditional flowers of the grave, delivered to the victim before the kill. The cadaver is dressed up and made up and laid down and ritually violated and consecrated to an eternity of being used." .... "Heterosexual intercourse is the pure, formalized expression of contempt for women's bodies."
(Andrea Dworkin).

Get this one:

"The male is a domestic animal which, if treated with firmness...can be trained to do most things."
Jilly Cooper, SCUM (Society for Cutting Up Men.)

Can you imagine a man saying **THAT** about a woman?

MALE: . . . represents a variant of or deviation from the category of female. The first males were mutants . . . the male sex represents a degeneration and deformity of the female. **MAN:** . . . an obsolete life form . . . an ordinary creature that needs to be watched...a contradictory baby-man... (From *A Feminist Dictionary*, ed. Kramarae and Triechler, Pandora Press 1985)

Women are the only oppressed group in our society that lives in intimate association with their oppressors.
(Evelyn Cunningham)

Why didn't all those oppressed women do something centuries and millennia earlier in response to the oppressive institution of marriage and the Patriarchy? They weren't oppressed by men at all, that's why. The oppression of women, if it occurred at all, was done by good old *Mother* Nature herself. Yup, that's right Mother Nature oppressed women by making them physically smaller and weaker than men. *Mother* Nature decided that women were the part of our species that would be fairly incapacitated in order to gestate a child for nine or so months inside her body. *Mother* Nature decided to give women and not men breasts capable of lactating in order to feed the offspring. Men didn't have squat to do with it. Why do you think feminists are hell bent on making abortion legal and keeping it that way? Feminists, if they are to succeed in "liberating" women have to negate the machinations of **Mother** Nature, evolution or God (take your pick, the end state is the same).

But who gets blamed for it? Men do. Men are the ones against whom all the vitriol and anger at God and nature are directed. Read the above quotes again and tell me if you see any references to the way nature actually dealt the cards. And men, being the fair guys we are, but mostly to get laid, agree to this crap. We go along with it, we *pretend* that we are all equal.

In any non industrial, agrarian society, where survival is a matter of coaxing food and shelter from the earth unassisted by machinery, gender roles are well defined along the lines of who is the most physically able and mentally suited to perform the labor. Only in an industrial or information based society does a weaker and less physically capable creature have the ability to express discontent at the way in which nature and Nature's God made them. In any other social arrangement, they are more often than not grateful that someone else is willing and able to do the hard, dirty and dangerous work of feeding and protecting them and they reward those who maintain their existence rather than demean them.

Feminism and the ideas of feminism have become so deeply ingrained into our collective societal consciousness that we hardly recognize it for what it is. Feminism is an enemy of men who actually want to be husbands and fathers. It is an evil that seeks to destroy the institution upon which societies are built, namely the family. This isn't my opinion; this is what the feminists themselves have said. Women in general have been taught this garbage in ways overt and subtle. They have soaked it in and it has become a part of their decision making process, their feelings and intuitions. In so doing, they have set up a no win situation for men. If we point out that Feminism is illogical and stupid, we are accused of simply proving the Patriarchy exists.
Feminism, by its own definition seeks to destroy the institution of marriage. Get this, whether you are married, divorced or single and looking, feminism is teaching women that marriage is a bad thing for them. They are being taught that you, the husband, boyfriend and lover are the oppressor and the enemy. All it takes is for you to act in any way that they disapprove of and you are simply proving the more radical feminists correct in their assertions about men. This is a no win situation for the men of Western Civilization.

You might say that the really radical feminists, the "feminazis" are the only ones who think this way and that as a general rule, your wife, girlfriend, etc, isn't one of those people. She might not be overtly and militantly feminist in her world view, but the worldview of feminism has so pervaded our culture that she has inevitably absorbed the feminist distrust and dim view of men in general.

Here are some more great quotes that illustrate the feminist meme and its attitude toward men:

"All men are rapists and that's all they are."
Marilyn French, Author; (later, advisor to Al Gore's Presidential Campaign.)

"All sex, even consensual sex between a married couple, is an act of violence perpetrated against a woman."   Catherine MacKinnon

"I feel what they feel: man-hating, that volatile admixture of pity, contempt, disgust, envy, alienation, fear, and rage at men. It is hatred not only for the anonymous man who makes sucking noises on the street, not only for the rapist or the judge who acquits him, but for what the Greeks called philo-aphilos, 'hate in love,' for the men women share their lives with--husbands, lovers, friends, fathers, brothers, sons, coworkers."   Judith Levine, *My Enemy, My love.*

"I feel that 'man-hating' is an honorable and viable political act, that the oppressed have a right to class-hatred against the class that is oppressing them." Robin Morgan, *Ms. Magazine* Editor.

Women are being taught to hate men and sex with men. Robin Morgan is the global editor for a women's magazine. Guess who reads women's magazines? Women do! Think this attitude towards men isn't reflected in popular culture? Watch an episode of *Everybody Loves Raymond* or the average commercial that portrays Dad as a dunce and get back with me on that. My eleven year old son was sharp enough to deduce that most prime time television is decidedly anti male and anti marriage. Remember when men were presented in a positive light on television, back before it pretty much became the idiot box?

I challenge you to do some research. Compare the increase in divorce rates in the Western world and compare them to the rise and acceptance of the feminist ideology. The results while alarming are not surprising.

Feminism has created a climate that encourages women to be sexually promiscuous before marriage, the notion of doing as they please with their own bodies, but it has also taught women that once married, the husband is to have no explicit access to the same body she was giving away to other men on a regular basis. If a woman is willing to turn her body over to her husband, he is somehow raping her. Wonder why the ex resented having sex so much, with *you* anyway?

Feminism has created an undercurrent of distrust and envy towards men. Men are portrayed at best as comically stupid buffoons to be pitied and mocked and at worst overbearing brutish control freaks.

Feminism has taught women that they don't need men, that men are the enemy, the oppressor. When a woman becomes disgruntled or bored with her role as the wife and mother, she gets a free pass via feminism to walk away under the blanket of feminism's doctrines of men are evil and marriage is oppression. Feminism gives women a reason to leave a marriage that hasn't fulfilled her ideals of Romantic love.

Still wonder why your wife found it so easy to leave you? Still wonder how she could destroy her family? Regardless of whatever excuse she might have coughed up, regurgitated for leaving you, the reason is the conflict between the impossible to live up to ideal of love she demanded from you and the intellectual escape hatch provided by feminism. You doubt me? Look at what a feminist said about the effect of feminism:

"The social and political agenda of the feminist movement expanded as the philosophy of the movement evolved. Women initially wanted to overcome their biological differences in order to be equal with (i.e. the same as) men. They thus sought legal freedom for abortion, changes in marriage and divorce law, tax reform, universal day care, pay equity, affirmative action in employment, and changes in language. In the second phase of development, their agenda expanded their attention from naming themselves to naming their world. They emphasized female strengths and women's capacity for love, acceptance, peace and empathy; and added issues such as ... homosexual rights, aboriginal rights ... Finally, feminism moved into a third phase of spiritual awareness. By the time feminism had reached its third phase of development, its earlier goals were well on their way to being realized. North American society had moved toward accepting an integrating the feminist view of abortion, day care, divorce, sexual liberty, and affirmative action into common policy. The agenda ... had also progressed toward mainstream integration. The mainstream acceptance of the feminist agenda caused the movement to lose its distinction. ... *Feminists are becoming difficult to identify, not because they do not exist, but because their philosophy has been integrated into mainstream society so thoroughly. The philosophy is almost unidentifiable as feminist, for it is virtually indistinguishable from mainstream,*" (pp. 250-251).

Mary Kassian, a former Feminist, *THE FEMINIST GOSPEL* (Crossway: Wheaton, 1992)

Turn on the television any night of the week and flip around the channels. Make a conscious effort to look for negative media portrayals of men and the masculine. Take the "please entertain me" glasses off for awhile, stop worrying if the woman watching it with you is going to have sex with you that night and look for the pattern of male bashing on the prime time television programs.

Dr. Macnamara, who works as a media researcher, conducted the research for his PhD at the University of Western Sydney. He has recently published his findings in a book, *Media and Male Identity: The Making and Remaking of Men*.

As part of the study, he undertook an extensive content analysis of mass media portrayals of men and male identity focusing on news, features, current affairs, talk shows and lifestyle media. Over six months, the study involved detailed analysis of over 2,000 media articles and program segments.

Dr Macnamara found that, by volume, 69 per cent of mass media reporting and commentary on men was unfavorable, compared with just 12 per cent favorable and 19 per cent neutral or balanced.

Some of the recurring themes in media content portrayed men as violent, sexually abusive, unable to be trusted with children, 'deadbeat dads', commitment phobic and in need of 're-construction'.

"Men were predominantly reported or portrayed in mass media as villains, aggressors, perverts and philanderers, with more than 75 per cent of all mass media representations of men and male identity showing men in on one of these four ways," Dr Macnamara says.

Further, in somewhat of a back-handed compliment, when positive portrayals of men as sensitive, emotional or caring were presented, these were described as men's and boys' 'feminine side.'

"Ultimately such portrayals could lead to negative social and even financial costs for society in areas such as male health, rising suicide rates and family disintegration," he warns.

'Media and Male Identity: The Making and Re-making of Men' is published by Palgrave Macmillan.

This brainwashing is pervasive and we as men and fathers are reaping the results of it.

Women instinctively know that on some level and in some ways they need men. Men will readily admit that they need women for a variety of things apart from sex. When men and women willingly acknowledge the inherent differences, the strengths and weaknesses Nature gave them, they get along wonderfully. When women apply the fairy tale script of romantic love to their relationship with you and you come up short, feminism tells them to dump you. Chances are if you very carefully reflect on your failed relationship you can recall instances that illustrate the forces of Romantic love's unrealistic expectations and feminism eroding your wife's love and respect for you.

Feminism teaches women that they can be "independent" and make it on their own and indeed they can. The cost of her sudden spontaneous independence once she realizes she isn't "happy" is usually a heart wrenching divorce and the destruction of a family that could have been salvaged if a big dose of reality had been injected into the situation. Men in the feminist world are merely accessories, breeders to be used to give career women children so as to satiate the biological urge to reproduce. All women who are leaving have a support group of other women who will tell her how much better things will be if she leaves her husband. These "you go girl" type of women are usually trapped in nightmare marriages of their own making or are divorcees themselves.

Now that we have briefly examined both Romantic love and Feminism, put the two next to each other and compare. Romantic love teaches that women are the center of the universe to be catered to by men in every way. Feminism teaches that women are the center of the universe and that men and marriage are the enemy.

Some will read this and assume that I am giving the men in the failed marriage a free pass. I am not doing this at all. Earlier I told the men whose wives left them that they needed to take a long hard look in the mirror. I still think that we as men need to be 100% responsible for the things we do to mess up our marriages. The point I am making is that from a cultural stand point women are encourage to leave the marriage. In the next section I will address how women who leave are rewarded by a system that needs to be abolished altogether.

It is not enough to for me to help you understand the "why" of the breakup of your marriage and family. Families are being devastated; children are being hurt emotionally and mentally by the incredible number of walk away wives. We know why our wives are leaving in droves to seek the elusive "one" that will meet the "need" foisted on their psyches by Romantic love. We understand the adversarial relationship and escape hatch mentality created by feminism. This trend isn't going to reverse itself anytime soon. We know that women are more likely to file for a divorce than men are. We know also that courts and "family law" both work in favor of the woman and deprive men of an inequitable amount of income and most importantly, access to our children. We as men will be hard pressed to reverse this trend any time soon. What we need is a way to protect our mental and emotional health, our children and our assets.

So, there you have it. She is leaving and now you know why. You also know how to take control of the situation and start getting your life back together. It isn't easy. I know. But trust me, you will survive this. You will go on and have a good life, and once the child support payments are finished, hopefully a prosperous one as well. The rest of this book tells you how to avoid it the next time.

HOW TO FIX IT

(CAUSE THAT'S WHAT MEN DO – WE FIX STUFF)

The gig is up. It is time for men to realize that they are playing with a deck that has been so stacked against them they have no way of ever being dealt a winning hand.

History of Marriage in Western Civilization

Just understanding why does us no good. We men, for the sake of our sons and daughters, need to restore order to the realm as it were. We need to readjust the system of marriage in order to compensate for the effect these two ideas are having on our civilization and on our families.

Being "in love" is not a good enough reason for getting married. Love or what we think love is fades over time. That "in love" Romantic love is replaced by one of two things. One of the things it is replaced by is a deep and genuine respect for the other individual in the relationship. That love may or may not be reciprocated. "In love" is replaced by concern and a desire to care for and meet the needs of the other individual in the relationship. As the "in love" chemical attraction fades, it can also be replaced by a type of loathing that only one who has experienced it, in either giving or receiving, can understand. If you are reading this book, you are one of those who have experienced love gone wrong.

63

You might be reading this and thinking, "Bill, I agree we need to fix this situation. But how do we do it?" I am going to propose some radical things that might help us repair this insanity. First I want to examine the institution of marriage from a historical point of view. Most of us look at history from a modern perspective. We apply our values to the people in history when we read or study it. This is kind of unfair to those who lived thousands of years before us and even hundreds of years before us.

We need to examine the institution of marriage so we can understand how it has somehow morphed into a system that no sane man will participate in. Think about it for a minute. Why would a man willingly subject himself to having sex with one woman the rest of his life when there is no guarantee that she will actually provide that sex? Why would a sane, rational man take on the responsibility of a family when he could loose that family at the whim of the wife? Why would a man sign a piece of paper that subordinates and enslaves him physically and financially to a woman with the State as the arbiter?

Modern marriage in Western Civilization is a combination of Roman and Germanic custom filtered through the religion of Christianity. Western marriage has also been influenced by the doctrine of the medieval Christian church, the politics of the Protestant Reformation, the Industrial Revolution and by attempts to regulate the marriages of people of different races in the United States. Marriage before the Advent of Romantic Love was the business of the two families which brought the future husband and wife together in an arranged marriage. Marriage was primarily an *economic* arrangement. Romantic Love rarely if ever entered into the equation.

In the early history of Christian Europe, marriage was a civil affair administered primarily by the families. Only as the Church gained increasing influence, did the view of marriage as an unbreakable sacred bond take hold in society at large. The Church decided that once married a couple could not be divorced. Note that God Himself did not say this, but the Church. Since divorce was no longer permitted, an annulment was the only way of dissolving a marriage. Couples soon found reasons to get those annulments by using the churches own regulations. The Church did raise the status of women by declaring that women and men could only marry under mutual consent. Before then, women were pretty much "bought" by paying the bride price to the father. Here we have the beginnings of a gradual process of removing the parents as the final authority on matters of marriage and the eventual transference of it to the individual and the State.

By the 12th and 13th centuries, the priests of the Church were the ones in charge of the whole "marriage" business. The Protestant Reformation of the

16th century changed all of this by putting the authority to regulate marriage in the hands of the State. Martin Luther, the great reformer, decided that marriage was "a worldly thing . . . that belongs to the realm of government", Calvin felt the same way and under Mr. Calvin, the requirement of State registration of marriage was genuinely introduced into our culture. The busy body Puritans brought the Protestant idea that marriage was a secular rather than religious affair to America.

In early America, the church and the family was the sanctioning authority for a marriage. Pretty much worked this way: two people got together, decided to marry each other, got the parents blessing, said some vows at church or in front of a minister and posted a notice in the town square no less than fifteen days after they began to cohabitate stating that they were indeed married. That's it. No divorce courts, no family law, no goofy notions of romantic love and no feminism.

The first marriage licenses as we now know them in the United States were an attempt to prevent blacks and whites from marrying each other. In effect, the State was deciding who would be able to get married based on criteria of race determined by the State. As it now stands, when two people go down to the court house and get a marriage license, they are entering into a legally binding contract with the **State**. Think about that for a minute, the State is the third party to a union of two people who are allegedly marrying for love and plan on a lifetime commitment. Finally, the State has come along and said OK, we are going to have no fault divorces. No one's fault really, things didn't work out, fill out some papers, talk to a judge and make sure that the property is divvied up and go on your way.

The question to ask is, "**who profits from divorce?**" Here we are, back to the money thing again. I once dated, well, we met for coffee once, a woman who told me in no uncertain terms that divorce as an industry was good for all other industries in the country. She was a realtor and related to me that a high divorce rate is good for her business. Why? A few years after a divorce, another house gets bought by one of the people who divorced. Almost non existent is the time when a man and a woman would buy a house and stay in it raising a generation or two of children. Who else profits from the incredibly high divorce rate? The businesses that furnish houses, the attorneys, the day care centers, the child psychologists and fast food joints, did I forget divorce attorneys?

As it stands now, men are at a distinct disadvantage when it comes to marriage and the subsequent divorce. Men are more likely to suffer financially, emotionally, physically and mentally when a woman chooses to leave her family. It is true that divorced women are more likely to live below

65

the poverty line than divorced men, initially, but thanks to a plethora of State programs, in a few years she has a job that puts her on par with the ex husband financially. For a man, the risk of financial ruin is nothing compared to the risk of being cutout of his children's lives. But for some reason Judges seem to think that the kids need mom more than dad and that mom not dad is usually the better care giver.

I firmly believe that the primary motivating factor for men to accept the monogamous marriage relationship is his desire to have a family. Why else would a man say sure, I'll stick with one woman the rest of my life. I believe that most men just want a family. He wants a place to come home to at night, a loving wife and healthy, happy children, his children. Modern society has made that desire almost an impossibility. Some will say that I am overly pessimistic. I would argue that with a 50% divorce rate I am merely recommending extreme and realistic caution.

We need to stop asking the state to enter into our marriage contracts. By asking the State to enter into the marriage contract, we have invited it to be the final authority over the dissolution of the marriage. I know, you think that you have to get a marriage license to make it a real marriage. NO YOU DON"T. When God put Adam and Eve together, did they go to the courthouse and sign a piece of paper before they were considered husband and wife? Nope. Don't buy into all the religion stuff? Did Ug the caveman and Uggette the cave girl have a marriage license? Nope. There is no real reason to enter into a contract whose potential ending is setting you up for emotional and mental torture and bankruptcy.

Here is what I propose:

Before deciding to *cohabitate*, go to an attorney and you and the woman draw up papers describing how you will divide the assets in the event that the two of you decide to end the relationship later. Each of you signs a paper stating that for moral and religious reasons you DO NOT want the State to interfere in any way, **ever**, with your relationship. Do what ever you need to in order to make this document as legally binding as possible. Once this is done, in order to make the arrangement morally and socially binding, have a public ceremony in front of witnesses. It can be just as meaningful and spiritually pleasing to whatever God you choose to worship without an official piece of State paper. Make it as much as possible, an economic relationship as far as the legalities are concerned. Love has little to do with property, especially at the beginning of the relationship. BUT, wait until the relationship ends and see how important the property becomes. All we are doing here is returning some common sense to the marriage arrangement. We are once again making it an economic arrangement, one in which the man is out to fairly protect himself, romantic love aside.

If you are religious, go to the minister or whoever, and say, "Listen preacher, we want to enter into a marriage covenant before God and witnessed by the church. We will NOT, in accordance with our interpretation of Scripture, invite the State into what is strictly a private and personal matter between the two of us. Will you officiate at the ceremony?" If he says no, find a minister who will respect your religious beliefs and perform the ceremony.

If religion plays no role in your life, find someone you respect and ask them to officiate or lead a ceremony and exchange of vows, just as you would if you were going to get married. If you would like, for a baloney sandwich and a bottle of good bourbon, I'll say a few words and you can exchange your vows in front of me.

After the "ceremony", religious or otherwise, she can legally change her last name to yours. Same results, except no State to step in when she decides she is no longer happy and all of a sudden you are no longer needed in her life.

If you own the house, keep it in your name and your name only. I recommend that you have her sign a lease, charging her a dollar or so a month, more if she has a job, to live there. That way, if she ever decides to walk, all that is legally happening is that a tenant is moving out. Since the divorce rate is around 50% there is a good chance that is all she will be eventually anyway.

What about the children we might have together?

Good question, you're thinking right along with me. Before the "marriage" tell her that if she leaves the relationship, for any reason other than you fathering a child with another woman, abuse etc, etc, whatever the two of you decide on, that she is not going to get anything in the way of your assets. Put it in writing; make it a legal document between the two of you. (Form a limited liability corporation if you have to for the purpose of producing common household dust.) When the child is born, she can list you as the father and give the child your last name on the birth certificate. Shortly after the birth, have a paternity test done. Agree to this years in advance so it is not an issue at the time. If the child is yours, great you can legally adopt them, giving you legal access to the child. If the child is **not** yours you can terminate the relationship immediately and assume no legal responsibility for the child. Insist that you will not pay any form of child support to the mother if she enters into a marriage or cohabitation arrangement with another man. You will of course agree to provide for your children when they are with you, but only when they are physically with *you.*

The idea here is that you are protecting yourself against future loss. You are simply entering into a mutually advantageous economic and social agreement. You might even want to include a list of duties and responsibilities each of you will perform, perhaps an agreement about the frequency of sex, the kinds of chores each will and won't do around the house. Perhaps you can agree to provide financially during pregnancy and for a year after childbirth. Whatever, just make sure you make all of these considerations without concern for the false and soon to fade idealism of romantic "in love", love.

It is time that men in general rebel in a real and meaningful way against a system that is penalizing us for wanting to have families. If after you consult with an attorney on this, you find that the laws of your particular State would make the outcome less than favorable for you, refuse to get married unless she agrees to move to a State whose laws are consistent with your desire to protect yourself.

She might resist this plan altogether. If she does, dump her. She might object and say something along the lines of, "Oh, you don't want to *really* marry me." Explain to her that as far as you are concerned it will be a marriage, between the two of you, excluding the State. If she insists on a State license after you have explained your reasons for not wanting one be careful, she already has the ever so tiny seed of divorce and financial rape growing somewhere in her mind.

APPENDICES

Appendix A: Divorce in the Bible

First thing you need to understand and practice when reading the Bible for guidance and instruction, is to read things in context. A lot of people will tell you, "God hates divorce." I think He does, but not because I took a few verses out of context to make the point. I will briefly examine each of the passages used to push the big guilt trip on guys when they are encouraged to "fight" for their marriages. There are two parts to the Bible, the Old and New Testaments. Let's look at what each one actually says and then tie the two together.

In the Old Testament, God was pretty quiet concerning divorce. In Ezra, a situation occurs where divorce is commanded in order to make things right with God. That's right, in essence, God commanded it, the same God religious people will use to shame you into not being glad about making peace with the upcoming heart wrenching divorce you didn't want in the first place. In Ezra chapters 9 and 10, the men had married Babylonian women during the captivity there. Once back in Jerusalem Ezra addresses this problem. Two whole chapters deal with this. In fact, there was a public divorce ceremony. Some will argue that God did this to make sure that the Israelites were not influenced by the paganism of Babylon by having a bunch of little idol worshipping wives at home and this situation is an exception to the rule. Really? Not what that Book says. No where in the two chapters in Ezra, dealing with the divorce, a bunch of divorces actually, in order to make things right with God and put away the foreign "heathen" wives they had taken during the captivity, does the Holy Spirit take the time to inspire the writer to say, "This is a very big exception to the rule and is a one shot deal."

But wait, doesn't the Bible say that God hates divorce? Yes, it does say that in Malachi chapter 2 and verse 16. But read the whole section and you will find out why. God hates "putting away" because the man was breaking a covenant with the wife of his youth. God certainly hates divorce, but He hates the breaking of covenants even more. So you have to ask yourself, who is breaking the covenant in your case. Is it you or is it her? If it is her, why are you the one worrying about God being upset at you? Why are you expending energy trying to convince God via prayer to bring a covenant, or holy contract, breaker back into your life?

Concerning divorce and the Law of Moses, the Bible says in Deuteronomy chapter 24 and verses 1-4 that if a man finds some uncleanness in his wife and she finds no favor in his eyes, he can write her a bill of divorce and send her on her way. BUT get this, if she goes off and becomes another man's wife, he isn't allowed to take her back, even if she divorces the other guy or the other guy dies.

Is your wife, the one who crushed your heart fooling around with another guy? You are treading on thin ice if you choose to take her back, you might, depending on your definition of what scripturally constitutes "marriage" be committing an abomination before the Lord.

In most Christian circles, divorce is considered a sin, except for cases of fornication. This comes from the words of Jesus in Matthew 5:31-32 and 19:3-9. The Pharisees, the teachers of the Law of Moses, the "experts" of the day came to Jesus and said, What about divorce? Jesus said in a nut shell, "God wanted it to be one man and one woman for life. God knows the hardness of your hearts, so He allowed for divorce. If one of the two fornicates, divorce is O.K. But the two can't get married again without committing adultery."

Chances are, if your wife is leaving you and you aren't a drunk and druggie or are beating her, she has a man on the side or is planning on having one. The most common reason given by women for leaving is that they are "unhappy" in the relationship. Unhappy people usually seek to find that happiness with someone or something else. Back to what the Bible says about divorce.

Further on in the New Testament, in the Letter Paul wrote to the church at Corinth and said that if the two people are believers, the wives shouldn't leave the husband. If she does, she should remain unmarried or be reconciled to her husband. The husband isn't supposed to leave his wife. If the man has a wife who isn't a believer and she wants to stay, the husband ought to let her and the same with the wife who has an unbelieving husband. BUT, if the unbeliever leaves, LET THEM. Are you getting this? If your wife walks out and she isn't a believer you need to let her go. YOU aren't under bondage in that case.

Now, let's add one more verse and tie it all together. Jesus and Genesis 2:24 both say that when a man and woman enter into a marriage covenant / contract and consummate it, the two become one flesh. What God has joined together, let not MAN put asunder. If your wife has trotted off to a human judge and filed for a divorce and gotten or is getting one, both she and the judge are the ones doing the wrong or sin here, not you. If your wife is not a believer, you need to let her go. If she is a believer and you want to take her back you can, UNLESS she has been with another man. This stuff is pretty straight forward and simple. Of course, someone will trot out "forgiveness" and tell you that in order to be like Jesus you need to forgive her and take her back. Maybe you ought to; I wouldn't personally recommend entering into any kind of covenant with a known contract breaker. Do you regularly do business with a know swindler or cheat?

In any event, if you were opposed to the divorce and wanted reconciliation, but your wife insisted on it, **you** have not sinned against God. If you are a religious person, a believer, I would recommend you give it over to your God and lay it at His feet. Let Him deal with your ex-wife in a manner that He sees fit. Wash your hands of her and move on with your life. None of this is meant to justify divorce. It is simply saying that God, in His wisdom and foreknowledge knew that humans would be getting divorces. While His plan was the permanence of marriage, God makes allowances for divorce.

Appendix B: On Women

How much trouble could I get into for this one? I want you to understand the mentality of the *average* modern American woman. Her wanting to leave you, her insistence on the divorce that is killing you is a culmination of the female meme running out of control. Understanding what she is thinking right now, her emotional and mental state is important to in order to understand how innocent you are in creating her "unhappiness", the unhappiness she is seeking to escape by leaving you.

Some women will read this and think I am dead wrong, or they will say I am a misogynist and a male chauvinist. Some will get angry, and call me names. However, I have spoken to hundreds of them in the writing of this book, I have spent hours reading what they write on internet forums concerning relationships, romance and the general attitude they now possess. If you doubt any of what I am going to tell you about them, go spend the time I did online looking for the common threads and patterns of thought. Eventually, you'll see it.

I suggest everyman reading this go out and get a copy of Rich Zubaty's book, *What Men Know that Women Don't*. This is an excellent book that explains some of the ideas here much better than I ever could. None of what I am going to tell you should be taken as an anti-dating or even anti marriage stance. It is simply based on the observations I have made. I know that most men will eventually begin to date again, will eventually even get married. In order to do this successfully, you need to understand how women think and operate. Once you understand these things, dealing with women becomes much less complicated and actually more enjoyable.

The average American woman is not happy. I mention this over and over again. Guess why? Women actually *aren't* happy these days. In a nation that provides them with more material goods, more opportunity, more deference and more recognition of them as independent, autonomous individuals than any society in the history of mankind, they still remain "unhappy". With a longer average life span than men and control of more than 50% of the nation's wealth, with rows and rows of book shelves filled to bursting on women's issues, they still aren't happy. As I spoke with divorced women, I heard the same thing over and over again. "It wasn't working out", "I wasn't in love with him anymore", "we just didn't get along" and "He was never going to change". Over and over again the same things were said. These thoughts all reveal some very basic insights into the character and mentality of women in our society.

These are general insights and not all women are always this way all the time. In fact, a good many women are fully aware that they act and behave this way and either seek to temper the attitudes discussed or in some cases, glory in them; either way, you as a man need to understand the programming and in some areas the natural inclination of women. If you encounter a woman in a social setting or find yourself dating a woman that portrays any or all of these attitudes and ways of acting and thinking, I recommend you dump her, and fast.

Women want control.

Women, who have been taught that they are smarter than men, think that they need to be the ones in charge. I mentioned popular media portrayals of men earlier in which men are inevitably seen as bumbling incompetents or as smart, but evil, corrupt and greedy. Seems amazing to me how we functioned as a society when men were large and in charge if these stereotypes are true. In short, they aren't. But, because we have been flooded with these images and memes, women think them to be true. Women *know* they aren't stronger than men physically and no smarter, but in order to feel like our *genuine* equals, they must in some way be superior. At first it was the notion that women are more kind and loving, and then it somehow morphed into being *smarter* then men. Adopting this stance, fully justifies in her mind the right to be in control of the relationship.

Once again, instinctively women know that they aren't any more smart or any more kind and loving or stronger than men, but they ignore that instinct and attempt to control the man and the relationship. Some men allow women the control they seek. There is a word for that kind of man. Inevitably, no matter how much power and control a man gives a woman in a relationship, she wants more. If the man totally surrenders that power, the woman begins to despise him, to think less of him as a man. When something goes wrong, she will refuse to recognize that her own actions were the cause and she will seek to blame the man. Eventually she will seek a replacement saying that the man doesn't support or understand her or that he isn't masculine enough. If the man exerts himself and refuses to surrender his power as a man, she will accuse him of being controlling or a control freak. Her internal animal is begging for him to be the Alpha male, the head of the pack, but she resists it with all of her might.

Women want *more,* always.

As I pointed out, the root word for maternal and materialism is the word "mater" or "mother". Look around you, who buys all of the "stuff" in this country? Not the things required for keeping and maintaining life, but the junk that fills up houses and department stores? Women do. Who wants to go shopping more often than not? Women do. Advertisers know this, that's why the target audience is women, not men. That's why advertisers are free to produce commercials showing women as smarter and savvier than men. No doubt we are a materialistic society; men have been caught up in this as well. It is a female mindset nonetheless. Women for the most part marry up. They will say that they don't care how much money a man has but that is a lie as evidenced by their actions. They do this because a man with more money can get her and the offspring more stuff. To be fair to the women, it is a good thing that women are the shoppers, if it were left up to heterosexual males to feed the United States' economic engine, it would collapse. Look at a single male's house and then look at a woman's. Men just aren't wired to decorate the house, have closets full of clothes and knick knacks everywhere. If we do buy something, it is a tool or a big recreational type object. Usually the recreational object allows us to mentally escape, in a bass boat for example.

One of the reasons women leave men is to find someone who can get them more "stuff". Don't believe me? Research shows that a woman is more likely to divorce a man after an extended period of unemployment on the man's part. Of course, they demand the right to have a job, to work outside the home, etc. even if there are young children, but if a woman is the primary bread winner in a relationship for an extended period of time, she begins to loose respect for the man and will in many cases begin to demean and belittle him. She might say she wants equality, but her actions and attitudes betray what she is saying. Eventually she will leave a man who is less successful than she is.

Women want things to be *nice* and *fair.*

This mindset goes back to the whole concept of power. Once again, women instinctively know that they are the weaker sex. In order to keep from surrendering power to a man, they will demand that he not exercise his natural power because to do so is not fair. Women will call the cops if you hit them, and they should, but they expect to be able to strike a man with impunity. Hit her, you go to jail, she hits you and you laugh at her she gets mad and hits you again. In fact, laugh out loud ever at a woman's physical, emotional and mental weaknesses and they get angry. But, yours are supposed to be held up for scrutiny and derision. This is fairness.

I was at the grocery store just last night and went up to the deli counter. I had just barely missed the deli guy turning off the heating element underneath the display case. Once the heating elements go off, the store isn't supposed to sell the food. I started talking to the guy behind the counter and he gave me a chicken wing. I had almost convinced the guy to sell me some of the leftovers when a woman walked up and started looking at the counter. The poor guy explained to her that the counter was closed and that he couldn't sell her anything. She went off on the guy. What did she say? "This isn't fair". "Oh, he (referring to me) gets a sample but I can't get anything?" The situation didn't matter, talking to the poor guy behind the counter like a human being didn't matter. All that mattered to this woman was what was "fair". She stormed off in a huff, cussing as she went. I apologized to the guy for causing him trouble and went someplace else to eat.

Notice how every kid gets a trophy for playing sports these days? Be it little league base ball or soccer, every kid who puts on a uniform and shows up, whether he contributes to the success of the team or not, gets a trophy. It's the female meme at work, the "fairness" meme out of control. This is why after working at a job she doesn't really need and after you working all week at a job that is statistically more competitive, dangerous and dirty than her job she will demand that you do half of the traditional female jobs and *all* of the traditional "man" jobs around the house. Because it isn't fair that she works at a job the family doesn't need and has to do all of the house work. She won't change the oil in the cars or kill the mouse or fix the clogged toilet. She expects the man to do those things. But, she will resent it if you don't help cook supper and do the laundry. Fairness isn't about what is actually fair; it is about what is "fair" to her.

It isn't "fair" that you get to work outside the house all day if she is a stay at home mom and she is stuck taking care of the kids, it isn't fair once she is out in the big wide world making money to buy unnecessary "stuff" that she still has to do all of the women's work. It isn't "fair" that the women, the gender with the teats equipped to feed the children have to be accessible to the infant, so we invented baby formula in order to allow us to drop the infant off at day care (baby jail) so mom could go out to work. It wasn't "fair" that men could be sexually active and not have to carry around a baby for nine months or so, so we invented birth control and made abortion legal. Women by and large refuse to accept the notion that life isn't, hasn't and never will be fair. They demand fairness on their terms and reality be damned.

What women *say* and what they consistently *do* over time are two different things. This is why men claim to not understand women. Women seem to have internalized certain things they deem to be the truth. More often than not, these "truths" are grounded in how they *feel* about a subject. Hard scientific, statistical, information doesn't matter to the average woman unless the data happens to coincide with how she feels about the subject. This is the much vaunted "women's intuition". A woman will act on her feelings regardless of the facts. If she doesn't feel loved by you, based on her own internal emotional processes, she will eventually leave you. It doesn't matter that you actually did love her, or that you were a good and faithful husband or boy friend. The reality of the situation is irrelevant. She will say she wants the two of you to have a good marriage, to raise a family, but she will ignore the realities of what it takes to do that in order to exercise a reality based on her emotions and feelings.

The concept of being "nice" goes hand in hand with what is "fair". When a woman levels an accusation that someone else is not a "nice" person, what they are really saying is that the other person won't succumb to what they deem as fair. In other instances it means that the other person won't let the woman's reality, the way they *feel* things ought to be, dominate or define the situation. This is why all the kids, regardless of skill level and contribution get a trophy. The women have decided, they *feel*, that their child is just as good as everyone else on the team.

Women hate to be wrong

Women know they are weaker and no smarter than men but can't stand to admit it. They will use all the feminine charm they can muster in order to get a man to take the blame once an argument is beginning to wind down and de-escalate if it is clear that they are in the wrong. Women will seldom if ever say, "I was wrong." If they do, part of it will still be your fault. They might be wrong, but you are more wrong. I have seen it a hundred times, especially on internet forums. Women simply will not say, "I was wrong" in a way that men can understand. If they get caught being wrong, they simply stop responding. In real life face to face situations, the woman will inevitably hold on to the anger that comes at being proven wrong and store it away for later use.

How many times have you, as a man, knowingly said, O.K, "I was wrong dear", when you know deep down inside that the woman was way out of bounds and dead to rights wrong? You know why? She had to be right and she knows that you know this. Reality doesn't matter to her, only that you

76

validated how she felt about a certain subject or event. At some point in her early life, usually before she was a teenager, she has internalized certain beliefs and emotions. Those beliefs and emotions are the basis, the touchstone, of her reality for the rest of her life. Facts will become inconvenient things to be disparaged and outright ignored. If you do attempt to argue from a point of reason and logic, and you challenge her reality, she will resent you for it especially if you are right.

Women will always seek out a strong, independent man, and then seek to ⬜tame⬜ him.

This truth goes back and ties together all of the things we have discussed so far. Chances are, if you have been dumped by a woman and you weren't beating on her, screwing other women out in the open and embarrassing her, If you were a normal decent guy, who took care of and loved his family and she left you, she has decided to finally give up on taming you. Same applies if you were just dating a girl and she dumped you or better dealed you. A woman has to tame you if she is to get access to "stuff", your exclusive genetic material, and your undivided attention and obedience to her reality. If she doesn't tame you, she knows you won't put up with much of her silliness once the chemically induced euphoria of being "in love" with her wears off.

Think I'm crazy about this taming stuff? Look at high school romances. The young men most in touch with the male meme are the guys into sports and cars. Both are about power and control, speed and winning. Look at how those young men act around their girlfriends. Here you have a big hulking 6'2 220 lb. bundle of muscle and energy, raw power on the playing field and he is being led around by the nose by a little scrawny, but *sexy*, girl. A girl who wouldn't last a second on the grid iron has control over this hulking athletic dynamo. She'll show up to all the games and cheer, she'll brag about her boyfriend's prowess, but she will be in charge of the relationship. The kid can bench press a Volkswagen and run like a gazelle burger on the Serengeti But he gets all weak and melts into the ground when she bats her eyes.

Look at the gear head and that relationship. He can tell you all you need to know about horse power and speed and transmissions and tires, he can, in his mind, see and understand the intricacies of a carburetor or transmission and has the dexterity and courage to get his tricked out car up to 100 mph on the road. Sitting next to him is a little, scrawny chick who doesn't know nearly as much about cars as she pretends to if she pretends at all. She is the one in control. Let him seek to exert his independence and she will dump him.

Women have several tools in the kit bag with which she seeks to tame men. These tools are primarily praise, guilt and sex. Notice how when a woman first falls in love with a man, she cannot say enough good things about him and she will screw him silly or promise to once they are married or she is sure she has his undivided attention. She is doing these things in order to get the man to commit to her and to her alone. In order for her to keep you once she has you, she knows that she has to tame the inner man or she will loose you to another woman once the "in love" part wears off and you recognize her true nature and her attempts to impose her reality on you. She will use praise, to tame you. She will tell all of her friends and the man how wonderful he is. He will be the smartest, best looking, strongest, etc, etc man she has ever met. She is counting on the fact that as a child, the boy's mother used praise and guilt to control the poor guy when he began to feel the first urges of manhood stirring in his soul. Mark my words, once a young woman starts to feel her control over a man she is in a committed relationship with slipping, she will attempt to get him to impregnate her. She has to, she can't physically control him, he is stronger than she is. She can't emotionally control him; he operates on logic and not emotions and "feelings". She can't mentally control him, he is at least as smart as she is and operates in a reality that is connected to factual observation.

The woman will use sex either giving it freely or withholding it, in order to exert control over the man. Sex and sex appeal is her primary tool in the kit bag. You think it is a coincidence that women spend millions and millions of dollars every year in order to stay thin, look young via make up and plastic surgery and dress as provocatively as they can. Not a coincidence at all, her way of staying marketable. What happens once a woman gets married and has a few kids? Unless she is in the work place, she usually lets herself go. If she is in the workplace and is still dressing to kill, she is still looking. She is usually using her sex appeal to get ahead or she is worse looking to trade up in the husband department.

Once she is sure the sex thing is played out and she wants no more children, if she is still interested in sticking around, she will attempt to use praise to get you to bend to her will. She will tell everyone how wonderful you are. She will give you love in the form of praise for what you do that she wants and she will **withhold** love in the form of praise when you displease her, just as she does with sex. If you do what she wants, she will say, "You are so smart" if things go wrong and it was her idea, she will say, "It's alright, it's not *your* fault".

"How could you!?" Have you ever heard those words come out of a woman's mouth? She doesn't really want to know the reasons you did what you did, regardless of how bad it really was. She wants you to feel *guilt* over what you have done or not done. It isn't about the action, the action is irrelevant. What is important is how the action affected *her*. It isn't about you at all. If she can get you to feel guilty about it, she can control you and get you to not do the action again. Her reality has been impinged upon by your actions, she must regain control over you in order to get you to fit back into her reality. Let's say you went on a three week bender, got drunk as you could, you finally come home and she says what? "*I* was worried about you." "How could you do this to me/us?" ('us' really means her) "Why would you act like this?" etc. etc. those all sound like noble sentiments, but the reality is she is less concerned about you and more concerned about the impact your actions will have on her. If she knows you well, which she does, she knows exactly why you did what you did. She is going to lay the guilt on pretty thick in an attempt to get you back under her control.

Wonder why some women never shut up and constantly nag and harp at the man in their life? Control is why. She is verbally assaulting the poor guy in an attempt to control him. She can't physically force him to do what she wants, so she attempts mental assault. There is a constant verbal bombardment in an attempt to force the man to bend to her way of doing things when and how she wants them done. If you see a woman that is a nag to her husband, I can almost guarantee she has expended the mechanisms of sex, praise and guilt. In a last ditch effort she has launched an all out verbal assault in order to gain control over the man. When it fails, she gets mad and lets him know it. If a nag suddenly gets quiet she knows she has lost. When a woman who was nagging stops, she is ready to leave the relationship and more than likely will.

How many times have you heard of a woman who was leaving a man say something to the effect of, "I love him, but I just can't live with him any more." What she was really saying was, "I love him, but I can't control him anymore." When a woman looses her power over a man, she will leave him. It might make her unhappy, it might make her sad, but in the end, she will leave and almost *instinctively* seek out a man she can control.

Some reading this might think me a misogynist, Let me be very clear here, I am NOT. I don't hate women at all; I do sometimes hate the way certain women act. I also do not believe that all women are consistently the way I described them in general terms above. I do think that if women are allowed to tame a man, to manipulate a man, to take total control of a relationship, they will. On some level, they are driven to attempt this, on another level, they are equally driven by their own natures to submit to men.

I believe for men and women to cohabitate peacefully over the long term, they need to understand their true natures and not the media portrayal of the genders. There are of course women and men who get it. The women who don't understand their natures are the ones to avoid.

I suggest you avoid women who left the last relationship they were in or if they divorced a husband, if they give any of the following as a reason:

They weren̄t happy. That is an indicator of a lack of spiritual depth and extreme selfishness. (Unless they realized how immature and dumb it was to leave for that reason)

The man was (allegedly) controlling. They will rebel against your natural role as the alpha male of the human pack (the family). These women usually recognize they are weak, but hate themselves for it. They seek to exert independence in situations where no one needs to be independent.

The man was over sexed. They will use sex as a tool to control you, guaranteed. This type of woman used sex at a certain frequency and intensity level to get the man and once she had him, she backed off. It made the man crazy and eventually he went elsewhere.

A woman whose ex committed suicide over the divorce, Wow, this is trouble and mucho guilt and baggage. You will be the surrogate she uses to absolve herself and it will drive you insane.

The man didn̄t love them enough. They will drain you emotionally and the love you show them will never be enough, usually this woman is extremely needy, clingy and emotionally immature.

The man didn̄t communicate well enough. What she usually means is that the man wasn't doing what she wanted, when she wanted and how she wanted. This one has to be right and keeps the relationship under the microscope.

She didn̄t love him any more. This woman, unless she has taken a big drink from the reality cup, won't love you any more at some point either. This one is especially pertinent for women who are divorced, but not so much for women who were just dating.

We grew apart. This is an admission that she got bored. Maybe he did too.

Are there some guys who are complete and total jerks? Sure. Do some men act the same way or exhibit poor behavior and downright cruelty to the women in their lives. Absolutely. But, I am not writing this for those guys. I am writing it for the men who can't figure out why they, a "good catch" can't seem to keep a girlfriend or who are losing a wife.

Avoid women in general if they:

Are angry at or badmouth all men except you

Are compulsive shoppers

Are overly interested in female celebrities

Are overly concerned about how much money you make

Are in a hurry to have children

Are obsessed with their careers

Constantly want to go have "fun"

Always want to go on a trip or vacation

Are addicted to television, especially reality television.

These are general guidelines to help you spot a woman whose world is all about her. Of course we men do have our faults and deficiencies in our natures as well. We *can* at times be too emotionally distant, we *can* be obsessed with sex, and we *can* be as materialistic and greedy as women can. But I argue that we are less likely to be this way especially the older we get. I would argue that most men have surrendered the nobler part of themselves in order to get access to sex. I would argue that most men are willing to be genuinely fair to women and will gladly trade a large dose of the Romantic Love women crave in exchange for a good wife and family not tainted by the Feminist meme.

I might be wrong about all of this and everything I've said, but I'll bet I'm not.

ABOUT THE AUTHOR

William Spriggs is a 22 year veteran of the United States Army. He has degrees in both History and Theology. This is his first and probably only book. He's got other important man stuff to do.